Contents

With deep appreciation to the pastors
and people of the North Heights Lutheran
Church, St. Paul, Minnesota whose love,
counsel, and fellowship have made many
stressful situations easier to bear.
Jan Markell

To my husband, Dave, who lovingly supported
and guided me as I made changes in my own
unbalanced lifestyle.
Jane Winn

1
Entering
the Stress Age

Inflation. Noise pollution. Energy shortage. Work pressure. Jet lag. These and other familiar by-products of our times are wearing us out, breaking us down, making us ill. As someone has put it, life in the '80s can be best described with three words: hurry, worry, and bury. But one word summarizes it all: *stress.*

Of the 10 leading causes of death in America today, 8 are attributed to stress. Experts agree that the average business executive has a 1 in 3 chance of dying of a heart attack by age 60. Unless we have an antistress program, our pulses probably beat more than 75 times a minute and that is dangerously high. Most of us have difficulty walking up 10 flights of stairs, and many of us are overweight or have cholesterol levels higher than 230.

It's not unusual to know several persons who have had heart bypass surgery. We're no longer shocked when men and women in their 30s and 40s drop dead of heart attacks. Many of our loved ones spend decades under the care of cardiologists.

A manufacturer advertises that life is getting tougher so his product is stronger. Book titles such as *The Beginning of the End, The Terminal Generation,* and *The Coming World Crisis* suggest that life *is* getting tougher. News magazines feature such articles as "Forecast: Earthquake," "To the Brink of Crisis," "Chemical Catastrophes," and "The Age of Disaster." Obviously, as well-informed people with no safety valves, we are going to suffer from *stress*. We may wonder where we went wrong, but the more important question is: How do we get out of the stress mess?

Stress—What Is It?

I remember the faddish '50s when families took a Sunday stroll to the corner drugstore for ice cream or sipped homemade lemonade on the front porch and watched people saunter by. Somewhere we stopped sitting together and became isolated robots in front of a television screen. Perhaps nothing has so drastically changed our lives as television. It broke up quality family time and generally destroyed intimacy. For some it creates stress; for others it relieves it. But what is stress?

According to Dr. Brian Briggs, a physician, stress is the body's response to any demand placed on it in which the body prepares to meet a threatening situation. In every such situation the body gets ready for flight or fight. Blood pressure increases, adrenaline shoots to the extremities, digestion slows, muscles tense. Dr. Briggs thinks life in the past 25 years has become so hectic our bodies are in stressful states most of the time.

It is normal to have stress in our lives, but we react differently to it. One person's stress may be another person's challenge. Heredity, personality, diet, state of mind, and training can alter the effects of stress. Used in a positive way it can spur us on in a crisis, or motivate and energize us. Unproductive stress, however, hinders our performance in life and dangerously interferes with our health. In fact, it can be deadly.

In his book *You Can Profit from Stress,* Dr. Gary Collins quotes Hans Selye, noted for his studies on the subject:

Stress is not simply nervous tension, nor is it something to be avoided or something which is always unpleasant. Riding a roller coaster, playing a game of tennis, or watching an emotional TV program can all be stressful, but these are stresses which we seek out and even enjoy. When it motivates us to action, stress can be good, but when it puts our bodies under prolonged physical and emotional pressure, then the very things which might have been stimulating and fun become destructive and unpleasant instead (Vision House, p. 4).

Nobody is exempt from this problem. Infants must cope with wet diapers. Children deal with parental discipline and sibling rivalry. Teenagers have pressures of peers, grades, the new morality, and choosing a career. Those in middle age may battle menopause, mid-life crisis, or children leaving the nest. Retirees deal with boredom, lack of self-worth, financial pressure, and failing health.

Add to any of these problems serious illness, death of a loved one, divorce, job change, transfer, financial loss, or shaky economy, and a serious stress attack is likely unless we provide safety valves to help us cope and control stress.

Our age is characterized by fierce competition, busyness, ambition, and aggressiveness. The race is against time and for success. Noise pollution, overcrowding, change, lack of privacy, schedules, dead-lines, budgets, and appointments further complicate our lives. We must take action to protect ourselves from destructive stress. I speak from personal experience. So does my colleague, Jane Winn, who is now a specialist in stress management in the Minneapolis area. I have written this book with Jane's input as well, that others may learn from our mistakes and develop a *balanced Christian lifestyle*. Only Christians with balanced lives can be positive witnesses for the kingdom of God.

The Prophet Daniel forecast that the latter years would be characterized by people "running to and fro" (Dan. 12:4). This, however, doesn't give Christians an excuse to be caught up in the current stress syndrome.

My Story
My intense battle with stress spanned a two-year period that had been precipitated by an unusually heavy ministry schedule. I am in Jewish evangelism where the laborers truly are few. Unwittingly I fell into the old "Messiah complex" snare. I sincerely felt that if *I* didn't preach the Gospel with intensity and win the lost, no one would. Several times a week I loaded my car with guitar, sound equipment, and literature,

and traveled hundreds of miles to proclaim the Gospel. Between road trips I pounded the typewriter to get out the message in print as well. My mind was never off the ministry and God's call to evangelize. If I wasn't working, I was thinking—always planning and coordinating projects. Seldom did I relax or enjoy leisure. People cautioned me to slow down, but instead I accepted more speaking engagements, explored book ideas, and mentally outlined a dozen new messages.

After five years of this I began to notice unpleasant symptoms that worsened over a two-year period. I was enveloped in fatigue that defies description. I had been an insomniac and knew tiredness, but this was all-consuming and debilitating, and was often worse after I awoke from an eight-hour sleep. I had headaches and dizziness, and my thinking was impaired. I lost weight and had little interest in food. Often I would drive away from my home and in a few minutes forget where I was headed. My jumbled thinking caused me to make many costly mistakes.

Jane Winn often cautioned me against the deepening stress syndrome she saw in my life. I paid little attention to her or to anyone, but instead explored other possible causes of the symptoms. Stubbornly I persisted with the ministry. I flew to Sioux Falls, South Dakota for meetings. As I labored through the first meeting, I sensed that things were about to come to an end. I held on to the podium, faked a smile, and forgot major points in my message.

Back in my motel room, I stared at the ceiling and realized I had spent nearly $3,000 looking for the cause of my symptoms. I knew I was unable to go through with the meetings in Sioux Falls or anywhere, and asked a friend in Minneapolis to cancel everything on my schedule for three months. As disco music from across the street further jarred my thinking, I knew I had to put on the brakes and revamp my lifestyle to include recreation, leisure, exercise, relaxation, rest, and good nutrition. My attitudes toward work and ministry had to change drastically.

As a result of my experience, I studied stress. The more I learned the more grateful I was that God had spared me from such other by-products of stress as arthritis, backaches, high blood pressure, cardiovascular disease, migraine, colitis, and mental breakdown.

More than 20 million Americans develop ulcers at some time in their lives, and 6,000 die yearly from ulcer complications. Twenty years ago only 1 woman suffered from ulcers for every 20 men. Today the ratio is 1 to 2. Now stress is also being linked to cancer. "We don't catch ulcers or migraine headaches. They come because our lifestyle encourages them. Stress weakens our bodies and makes us more susceptible to ailments," says Dr. Briggs. "In fact, medicine now attributes about 90 percent of illnesses to stress, tension, anxiety, or depression. Stress depletes our body of vitamins and complicates our immune system. Let's face it: dozens of diseases have disappeared in the 20th century, and yet hospitals are more crowded than ever. A century ago bacteria were considered the cause of all diseases. It is safe to say that stress is a major contributor to illness now as it actually causes changes in the metabolic functions and the body's defense system."

Never have I experienced stress more vividly than the night I went to check my parents' home while they were in Florida. As I unlocked the front door I found it was already open. My heart pounded. I could smell cigarette smoke. Someone had been in the house, and could still be there.

As I debated what to do, my breathing quickened and my hands were clammy. I turned on the light and hesitantly entered. The house was a disaster. Drawers had been opened and emptied, and radios, televisions, and musical instruments were gone. Cold air was blowing in the back door which had been kicked in. By then my knees felt weak and it seemed as if there was a knot in my stomach. Rational thinking was almost impossible.

Dr. Briggs later explained what was happening to my body during that stressful time: The brain perceived the stress and a message was transmitted to the hypothalamus gland which sent impulses to the pituitary gland. The pituitary released hormones which stimulated other glands. These glands then released other hormones such as adrenaline. The constant presence of stress hormones is dangerous. They wear down the body's immunological system and make us susceptible to diseases.

At that moment of extreme stress my body might have been unable to eliminate a mutant cancer cell had it been there. The presence of stress hormones caused great wear on my system.

As I hesitated between fleeing or calling the police, more was happening to my body. Dr. Briggs said my heartbeat increased to pump blood throughout the necessary tissues with greater speed, carrying oxygen and nutrients to cells. My blood pressure probably rose and my breathing became rapid and shallow. The liver released stored sugar into the blood to meet the increased energy needs. The blood flow to the digestive organs was constricted, but was increased to the brain and major muscles. All muscles became tense. The blood flow to the extremities was constricted, causing my hands and feet to be cold. The body perspired to cool itself since the increased metabolism generated more heat.

Stress will ultimately hinder thinking, weaken the body, make us prone to illness, agitate emotions, reduce our efficiency, dull our memory, and make us irritable.

The Christian has a unique type of stress. We want our ministries to be fruitful and our example to an unbelieving world to be right. Christians with legalistic backgrounds are constantly concerned that they not do the "don'ts" and always practice the "do's" of the Christian life. Doctrine can become dogma. Guilt and stress frequently lick at the heels of the Christian, and too often we've opened the door and invited them in.

Consider the Lily

Jesus taught that we should not be anxious (hassled, overworked, burned out, stressful). "Observe how the lilies of the field grow," He said. "They do not toil nor do they spin" (Matt. 6:25-28).

When we consider a lily we realize that it is beautiful being what God created it to be. It does not fret over what it might become or what it has not accomplished. It simply abides, lifting its face to the sun. We would be wise to lift our faces to the *Son,* but the busier we are, the more involved and successful we become, the harder it is to consider the lilies, let alone look to the Son.

One reason we "toil and spin" is because of the times in which we live. We're insecure. Jesus reminds us, however, that the Father knows we need food, clothing, and other necessities. He is aware of *all* our needs, and those of our ministries.

"The basic issue in a stressful life is wrapped up in the question: 'Who's in charge here?' If the answer is 'I am,' stressful living is present. Without the Spirit of God in control, we become tense. In His Spirit we are relaxed. We can explain to Him everything we have done, didn't do, or don't know how to do, without punishment" (Don Osgood, *Pressure Points: How to Deal with Stress,* Christian Herald Books, p. 33).

Jesus concluded His teaching by saying, "Each day has enough trouble of its own" (Matt. 6:34). Things haven't changed, have they? Each generation has anxieties. Unless we keep the physical, mental, and spiritual aspects of life in balance, we're headed for trouble.

Jesus said, "Fear not, little flock; for it is your Father's good pleasure to give you the kingdom" (Luke 12:32, KJV). God really wants to give us kingdom living—not stress-saturated living. In the Book of Isaiah we are reminded that the Lord will "continually guide [us] and satisfy [our] desire and . . . [we] will be like a watered garden, and like a spring of water whose waters do not fail" (58:11).

Jesus also taught that the meek would inherit the earth. Meek persons do not strive; they are not out to be number one, nor are they filled with aggressiveness. They simply abide. We can be delivered from the tyranny of stress when we adopt the lifestyle Jesus recommends.

The Balanced Life
If we don't learn to handle stress properly, individuals, families, and ministries will continue to break down. Believers freed from stress can better reach out to a stress-saturated world with the liberating news of Jesus. Unbelievers need to see us living healthful, balanced lives. Unfortunately, the world too often sees us struggling with fatigue, anxiety, depression, and worry. They see many of us overweight and out of shape, irritable, impatient, forgetful, angry, afraid, and hard to deal with.

It has been said that Christians "worship work, work at leisure, and play at worship" (Gordon J. Dahl, *Work, Play, and Worship in a*

Leisure-Oriented Society, Augsburg, p. 12). Through this book Jane and I want to help Christians get a perspective on the balanced life, to pinpoint stress, to understand what it does, how we can control it, and how we can make it work for us.

Too many of us are literally destroying ourselves because of unbalanced lives. Some of us are mistreating our bodies and may not know it.

Concrete Canyons

City sounds!
They're shattering me, Lord,
   and vibrating through my head.
They're bouncing off skyscrapers,
   multiplying 10 times 10 in decibels.
Could it be a plot
   to distract me from
   concentrating on You today, Lord?
From concentrating on Your
   serenity
   peace
   and order?
A plot to confuse me and to keep me from
   focusing on Your perfect direction
     for my life?
And on Your gentle words of daily comfort?
My generation is afraid of silence, Lord!
Our companions are tension, speed, and noise.
Oh, to hear the grass grow,
   or the flutter of the butterfly's wings.
Lord, I'm listening for Your still, small voice
   over the deafening din of modern-day progress,
   and the daily miracle is
   that Your voice comes through
   in spite of all the confusion!

Amen.

2
The Makings
of Madness

To know exactly how and why we entered the stress age would require an in-depth psychological and sociological study, but even in a casual look back we see trends. Busyness became a sign of success. We moved from the front porch to the back patio, safely behind our high fences, away from our neighbors. We broke the fellowship of the family dinner and began to eat in shifts. Fast-food places came along to capitalize on our frantic pace.

Madison Avenue has bombarded us. The hard-sell people have convinced us that we are not complete if we haven't bought their products. Twenty-five years ago they sold many on the idea that we should move out of the city to experience "the good life" and there was a mass exodus to the suburbs. Many invested in a ranch-style or split-level home with a two-car garage. Of course we had to *use* the two-car garage, so we purchased a second car, and besides, we no longer could walk or take a bus to our destinations as we did in the heart of the city.

To afford that new home and second car, husbands worked a little overtime, or wives got part-time jobs. As we earned the money, we found we liked to spend it. By then a subtle philosophy called "keeping-up-with-the-Joneses" had gained momentum in our society. We were neatly tucked away in our suburban cul-de-sacs and suddenly it mattered whose lawn was the greenest and whose had the fewest weeds. And since our neighbors were going up the "ladder of success," it mattered who made it to the top first.

The "Good Life" Expands

Madison Avenue quickened its pace, and the consumer became a pawn in the battle for the dollar. Soon we were also addicted to keeping up with the purchasing power of our neighbors. We rushed out and bought an electric toothbrush, pulsating shower head, food processor, designer jeans (new every year), a snowmobile, camper (Whatever happened to the tent?), a 10-speed bike, a waterbed, electronic games, transistor radios, pocket calculators, tape decks, a CB radio, jogging suits (What's wrong with old clothes?), blow combs, video recorders, and hundreds of other "good-life" products.

We entered the technological age.

Man's domination through technology has ironically enslaved him. It has projected him into his world and yet withdrawn him from it. The air conditioner spares us from the uncomfortable contact with the heat of the day; antiseptic hospitals quarantine out of existence, or at least out of sight, the miracle of so many realities like birth, suffering, disease, and the inevitability of death. One of the most frequent and proud claims made for many products today is that they are 'untouched by human hands.' The human hand had once been so eloquent, expressive, versatile, and constructive. It was used to touch, caress, plant and reap, sew, feed, soothe, carry, defend. The human hand does not do many of these things anymore. It is merely used to push buttons, pull strings, throw switches, and steer wheels (John Powell, S. J., *A Reason to Live! A Reason to Die!* Argus, p. 39).

The hassle doesn't end with the purchase of these items. We must make room for them, send in warranties, learn to operate them, even take classes on how to use them. Nothing is simple anymore. We've become the how-to generation with a book on every subject to help us keep up with the technology of the good life. We don't really own our timesaving gadgets: they own us. We buy these conveniences to make our lives easier and yet we have less time than ever to enjoy them.

Technology has taken its toll on us. A century ago we weren't as out of shape and stress-saturated. Today we don't split wood, shovel coal, or wash clothes on a scrub board. We push a vacuum cleaner, while our ancestors put the rug out on the line and beat it. Richard Keelor, Director of Program Development for the President's Council on Physical Fitness and Sports says: "In 1850, human muscles provided one-third of the energy used by workshops, factories, and farms. Today that figure has dropped to less than one percent" ("Ease Back into Shape," *Prevention Magazine,* Feb. '81, p. 146).

The Pace Quickens
John Powell accurately describes today's world as having new rhythms but no rhyme.

The once naked eye of man is now empowered by the remarkable vision of television, x-rays, telescopic lenses, radar cameras, and electronic microscopes. His ears have been scientifically sensitized by stethoscopes, cardiographs, seismographs, and magnetic tapes. His muscles have been amplified by all kinds of power equipment: power-driven machinery, power steering . . . laser beams, and guided missiles. His frail memory is enormously enlarged by Polaroid cameras, tape recorders, computers, and libraries on microfilm. . . .

The pulse and rhythms of human life have quickened so suddenly that all who want to keep up must run. To what we are running we cannot be sure, but we are making record time.

While our philosophers meditate on these new problems, the whir of life goes on. Spanking new expressways are drawing new lines of mobility across our country. Traffic engineers have put calculated curves in these expressways to save us from the periods of hypnotic dozing at the wheel. We don't have to look for landmarks, since many of them will have been bulldozed between our journeys, but we have only to keep reading those green signs that flash in our upper peripheral vision. We have only to streak along in our space-age crafts, trying to stay in our galaxy, right along the modern asphalt ribbon. . . .

Sometimes it seems that this highly mechanized, jet-propelled, staccato-tempoed technopolis is moving man closer and closer to a national nervous breakdown (*A Reason to Live*, pp. 14-15).

Man is discovering so much of his world that he is losing meaningful contact with it. He is gaining an increasing mastery over the forces of nature and at the same time he is becoming more and more alienated or separated from it. He is simultaneously becoming a master and an exile (p. 38).

Mixed Blessing

In the last 25 years there has been the explosion of knowledge, prophesied in the Book of Daniel as characteristic of the end times (Dan. 12:4). Some think that increased knowledge has made life easier, but it is a mixed blessing. Now we are expected to know about everything. We no longer have the option of being uninformed, so now we're hooked on the nightly news which constantly expands to greater coverage. Keeping up with one national and international crisis after another is wearing. Commentators warn of ominous days filled with economic peril and other stress-producing uncertainties. We become angry as we see the mistreatment of the world's poor, the hoarding and price gouging of oil, the taking of innocent hostages. In trying to keep up with the issues, we easily become depressed, angry, and stress-saturated.

Many issues today are volatile. Everyone feels strongly about such subjects as abortion, gun control, and busing. We can't sit on the fence any longer. We must be informed and able to defend our positions.

Some greedy manufacturers have turned out inferior products and, in order to protect ourselves, we have been forced to learn about vitamins, cholesterol, nutrition, insulation, cancer-causing substances, home repairs, and investment schemes—to name a few. We check out how-to books and manuals on every subject from marriage to losing weight, from car repairs to child rearing. Conflicting methods, ideologies, and philosophies bombard us, adding to stress. Airplanes are noisier. The neighbor's stereo makes the walls vibrate, and even his dog barks louder.

The credit card is claiming stress victims by the millions. Gone are the days when the family saved up for something special. Now we charge it and when the bill arrives wonder how we will pay for it. If we get even a month behind in payments, the pressure is on. Some stores won't let us buy too much for our income, but others will, and the interest mounts. A leading department store in Minneapolis admitted that it makes more money on interest than on *everything* else it sells.

Reaching for Success

The whole "success trap" heightened in the 1970s when income skyrocketed. Unions were successful in demanding and receiving sizable wage increases. Cars got bigger and more gluttonous. College costs began their steady rise. Madison Avenue advertising became more slick at promoting the symbols of success and affluence that everyone wanted.

"We are all reaching for success . . . whether a homemaker trying to nurture a family, a college student trying to obtain the right degree, or a person about to retire who doesn't know how to face the next several years" (Don Osgood, *Pressure Points, How to Deal With Stress,* Christian Herald Books, p. 143).

American society is obsessed with success.

The 1970s were called the "me" decade and the "doing my thing" decade. We sought position, power, identity, our rights, and an inflation-producing salary. We wanted to beat the system, get all that we deserved for as little as possible, to look out for "number one" and climb to the top no matter whom we trampled on. Society became the survival of the biggest.

The '70s wound down and the stress wound up as we worried about our future. Job markets became unpredictable and lifelong positions suddenly were in danger. We faced the possibility that the American dream could fade away. We were mortgaged and financed to the hilt. A shaky economy was jeopardizing everything and the stress factor began to push itself off the charts. Taxes went even higher and inflation consumed savings.

Watergate, Koreagate, Abscam, and other government fiascos reminded us that there was political instability as well as social and economic instability, and we wondered whom we could trust. All this brought change and nothing produces stress like change, whether it is reorganizing, repositioning or reevaluating.

People cry for peace in the sense of less turmoil, uncertainty, fear, and change, but there is none (Jer. 8:11).

Multiply one day's crises by 365. Add financial strain, inflation, traffic jams, unemployment, unplanned pregnancies, failure at school, obesity, smog, surgery, loneliness, alcoholism, drugs, and death. Subtract the support of the family unit. Divide by dozens of different opinions . . . and you come up with a formula that has the makings of madness. Block all avenues of escape and you have an enormous powder keg with a terribly short fuse. Even if you are a Christian . . . and love God intensely . . . and believe the Bible . . . and genuinely want to walk in obedience (Charles Swindoll, *Three Steps Forward, Two Steps Back,* Thomas Nelson, p. 14).

What, then, is the Christian's response to all of this? We're not to be pressed into the world's mold, but to recognize our unique call. Paul tells us that Christians are in a race, but that we all win! The world may battle for promotions and prestige, but we're to pick up one another and help one another.

And yet even Christians are not free of stress. We have a unique kind of stress—one that specializes in destroying the believer. We'll look at that in the next chapter.

Be Still and Know That I Am God

Lord, can I really go through life devoid of fear?
Another government toppled today.
The nightly news is only for those who thrive on human misery,
  it seems.
With each morning,
  I find it more difficult to be glad and rejoice in the new day!

But Lord, I desire to be thankful for all things,
  and so I need divine wisdom that shows me how You are
    working
  in spite of
    monetary crises
    double-digit inflation
    shady political deals
    back-stabbing international schemes
    and this mind-boggling dog-eat-dog atmosphere!

Rule and overrule, Lord.
Salvage what You can,
  and give me the insight to see the Master plan,
  and the behind-the-scenes intervention of Your hand
  on Planet Earth.

Amen.

3
Christian
Burnout

The world's code and the Christian's code are sometimes far apart. The world often lusts for power, money, success, pleasure, and revenge. Get all you can out of life. If someone hurts you, hurt him back. Blessed are the tough, rich, strong, and powerful.

In God's kingdom, the meek are called blessed. The Christian attempts to love his neighbor as himself, to turn the other cheek, and to focus more on the needs of others.

Such a philosophy does not guarantee a stress-free life. Christians often are victims of a unique kind of stress, and it is as deadly as the world's brand.

Though Jesus tells us not to worry or be anxious, most of us don't heed His words. He says, "Come to Me all you who are weary and burdened [exhausted from the rat race of life] and I will give you rest. I am gentle and humble and you will find rest for your souls. . . . For My yoke is easy and My burden is light (Matt. 11:28, 30, NIV). He wants us to delight in handing Him all our burdens. He didn't commission us to be tired, depressed, and angry burnouts.

We remind one another that Jesus is coming back soon and much of the world still needs to be evangelized. We look at the needs for teaching and restoring hurting people and we set unrealistic goals for ourselves. We are busy seven days a week, even though God Himself

23

worked only six days. The task of "saving the world" can be so stress-producing that more guilt and anxiety are produced than anything else.

The risk of burnout exists for all who dare to show compassion and are willing to help others. It is an occupational hazard as we try to live out the Gospel in a world that is lonely and starved for love. We are an easy target because of our zeal. We start out enthusiastically for God, but we don't acknowledge our limitations and along the way we break down. Satan may even lead us into a burnout schedule because he wants us out of commission for a reason.

I seldom took off a whole day. If I squeezed into my schedule a luncheon date with a friend, my mind was often on the ministry and on the next day's work. I saw so much to do and not enough willing workers.

Self-imposed Deadlines

Since I was single, I rationalized that I should put forth more energy than most people. I had no one at home demanding my attention, and after all, wasn't God my husband? I was determined to serve Him on a full-time basis and that meant no less than 80 hours a week.

I seldom slept well because my mind was constantly in gear, planning for the ministry. I was always outlining a new message, studying new books, keeping up with a dozen appointments during a week. My quiet time with the Lord suffered because my heart was never quiet. It was always focused on *self-imposed* deadlines.

When I began to sag a little, I stubbornly pushed myself even harder. The weariness was both physically and emotionally based, and it steadily worsened. Impatience and irritability were prominent. I frequently blamed others for the dilemna I had brought on myself. I was a perfectionist and became frustrated when others couldn't measure up. I was sure few could do the job quite the way I could—and that made me a sure candidate for burnout!

I felt bitterness toward my colleagues. They didn't work as hard as I did, or stay as late or cover as many miles as I did. They didn't thank me enough times. My constant unhappiness further drained energy. Insomnia, headaches, and allergy attacks were frequent. I was overly sensitive, had a negative outlook toward everything and everyone, and I cried at unexpected times.

I became disoriented. Recalling names and dates was hopeless. Concentration was impossible. Even listening to a good sermon was useless because my retention was so poor. I was consumed by "the ministry" and knew nothing of the rest of the people of God. "There remains, therefore a Sabbath rest for the people of God. For the one who has entered His rest has himself also rested from his works, as God did from His" (Heb. 4:9-10). God invites us to stop striving and gives Himself as an example of One who took time for rest.

My lifestyle didn't glorify God and it probably discouraged some people from following the Lord, for I was usually too tired to be a positive testimony for anything—especially the "peace that passes all understanding" (Phil. 4:7).

The Apostle Paul acknowledged that the Christian life can be a stressful experience. "We live in constant danger to our lives because we serve the Lord . . . Because of our preaching, we face death" (2 Cor. 4:11-12, LB). Consider what he went through:

Five times I received from the Jews 39 lashes. Three times I was beaten with rods, once I was stoned, three times I was shipwrecked, a night and a day I have spent in the deep.

I have been on frequent journeys, in dangers from rivers, dangers from robbers, dangers from my countrymen, dangers from the Gentiles, dangers in the city, dangers in the wilderness, dangers in the sea, dangers among false brethren; I have been in labor and hardship, through many sleepless nights, in hunger and thirst, often without food, in cold and exposure. Apart from such external things, there is the daily pressure upon me of concern for all the churches (2 Cor. 11:24-28).

There is hardly an adversity that Paul did not face, and he had a "thorn in the flesh" besides (2 Cor. 12:7, KJV).

His tone however, indicates that while we may be knocked down in the Lord's service, we're never knocked out. We may lose a battle or two, but we will win the war. Through it all, God never leaves us. He warned us that His followers would be like sheep among wolves; they would be persecuted and deprived of many of life's comforts. Above all, Jesus reminds us that He has overcome the world; that He gives a peace that the world cannot know; that He will never leave us.

Come Apart or You'll Fall Apart

Jesus knew what the stress-filled life was all about, even in His relatively slow-moving generation. Excited and sometimes frantic crowds often surrounded Him. On one occasion people had to be lowered through an opening in the roof to see Him (Mark 2:4). Crowds of more than 5,000 gathered to hear Him, to be healed, or to be delivered of demons. Yet the Gospels never paint a picture of a hurried, striving Jesus. Jesus even told His disciples to come apart and rest awhile! He frequently went by Himself to pray. Other times He took His disciples with Him and got away from it all.

If Jesus didn't have to be everything to everybody all the time, why should we? Jesus had His priorities in order. He recognized the Father's will as the most important aspect of His life. He maintained a steady devotional life with the Father. He ministered on a full-time basis, but He kept His life in balance. He took time "to consider the lilies," to smell the flowers, as we say today. The Bible indicates He rested and ate, and He certainly exercised, as walking was the primary way to get around in His day.

Another area of stress unique to Christians occurs when we are concerned whether we're doing the don'ts and not doing the do's. Guilt may be added to concern if we are participating in practices that are not glorifying to God. Real stress results.

Too often, however, when someone attempts to counsel us on a questionable practice, the counselor's spirit of accusation makes us afraid to discuss our problems or sin. Instead, we keep it to ourselves, and that not only produces stress, but we go on as defeated Christians. Those who counsel must do so lovingly. "Brethren, even if a man is caught in any trespass, you who are spiritual, restore such a one in a spirit of gentleness; each one looking to yourself, lest you too be tempted" (Gal. 6:1).

I have a Christian friend who feels hopelessly addicted to cigarettes. Try as she will, she has not been able to give them up. When she attends her weekly Bible study, she feels like a second-class

Christian. She is sure no one will understand her problem. Though some in the study group obviously indulge in too many calories (and the Bible is specific about the sin of gluttony), she senses that her smoking problem would be looked on as wicked. One Christian friend naively said to her, "Why don't you just stop?" *Just* stop. The one who gave this simplistic advice showed no understanding of what is involved in breaking an addiction. Such remarks keep my friend from enjoying full fellowship with Christians. She dreads the onset of Tuesday night because she feels stressful and guilty around other believers who are hindering rather than helping her to the more abundant life Jesus offers (John 10:10).

The do's result in stress too. Do we maintain good church attendance—Sunday night as well as midweek service? Do we always get the kids to Sunday School? Do we serve on enough committees? Do we use the right words when we pray aloud? Are our daily devotions pleasing to the Lord? (And are they even daily?) Are we less of a Christian because we don't have time to take a casserole to a bereaved family in the church? Did we properly greet all the visitors on Sunday, and invite some of them for coffee?

Are we witnessing? Is anybody responding to our witness? Or have people rejected the Gospel because they have seen what we're really like?

On and on we question whether or not we measure up in the kingdom of God. Often we want to measure up more for other people than for God. If we only could learn that when we desire to be *God-pleasers*, there is much less stress, for His yoke is easy and His burden light (Matt. 11:30).

Then there is the matter of tithing. Unbelievers cannot comprehend that Christians set aside certain amounts of their incomes for the Lord. New Christians are uncertain that they can keep up with their monthly bills if they give 10 percent or more of their salaries back to God. One protested strongly to God: "But, Lord, why do You get more than I do?" She felt God should get 10 percent of her income, but only after her bills were paid and she kept a little for herself. That way she didn't have 10 percent to give. Eventually she learned that God replaces what He takes and usually multiplies it in the process.

Till we've seen Him prove His faithfulness in this area, we may find it hard to let go of that 10 percent off the top.

Another aspect of money-management that leads to stress is the widespread use of credit buying. Christians too are guilty of charging more than they can pay for, and then they worry about what to do when the bills come in. Sometimes getting out of debt requires refinancing and months or even years of paying off. This puts added stress on the family as it tries to cope with inflation, recession, and—worst of all—the threat of unemployment.

Family Opposition

Some new believers experience stress because of family opposition to their new faith. I've been in Jewish evangelism a number of years and in this work such reaction is not unusual. Unbelieving Jewish parents have told me they would rather their kids be on drugs than follow Jesus. These parents may tolerate all sorts of behavior—even occult activity—but they will reject their child for following Jesus.

I'm learning, however, that Jewish believers are not the only ones who come under great stress when they become Christians. Others also risk the loss of family, friends, and loved ones. One of my close associates has been nearly disowned by his family because he had a born-again experience with the Lord. His family members are all churchgoers who insist that his confirmation was all he needed for salvation.

I've counseled many new believers who have agonized for weeks or months about how to tell their families about their newfound faith. Some have actually become physically ill or demonstrated serious emotional symptoms. This makes sense when we realize that one of the biggest stress producers is rejection by a loved one. New believers are frequently cut off from their most meaningful relationships. If they're not cut off, they may receive a cool reception each time they see a loved one. While not actually ostracized, they might as well be. If there is communication, what they believe is challenged and their new lifestyle is often criticized and misunderstood. They feel only hostility or irritation from those who mean so much to them.

Hand in hand with this is stress resulting from the concern they have for those loved ones. How can they reach them with the Gospel? Should they only pray or should they also boldly confront them with the message of Jesus?

I remember working closely with a young doctor who gave his heart to the Lord. His Jewish family was distraught. When they realized they were not going to persuade him to renounce the Lord, they cut him off from the family. They hung up on him when he telephoned and returned his mail unopened. There was serious talk about having a "funeral" for him.

When these efforts failed, the younger brother became so depressed that he tried to commit suicide in a last-ditch protest over his brother's new faith. Finally, the new convert's stress became so great as a result of the family's pressure that he renounced the Lord and pursued Orthodox Judaism instead.

His story is extreme, but every day new believers face various kinds of rejection. Through the centuries, followers of Jesus have experienced varying degrees of rejection. Since this will always be the case, Christians must learn to live with it and the stress that often accompanies it.

Rejection often leads to persecution. We read in the Bible that we can count on it (2 Tim. 3:12). In America there is detente between the forces of good and evil. We're experiencing little blatant persecution, but we may not be exempt forever. As we move more and more into the end times, this detente will come to an end and a new wave of intensified persecution will come. It may not include inquisitions, torture, and death, but it may. Any kind of threat to our well-being and safety is extremely stress producing. We need to learn how to handle stress in preparation for a world in which there will be an acute shortage of goods and food, intense persecution, and even the rise to power of a madman who will require everyone to have a number in order to buy and sell (Rev. 13:16-17).

Sound alarmist? This is what the Bible foretells. Many believe that the Christian will escape the worst persecution, but we should be prepared. According to the Bible, end-time pressures will be severe, and the Christian, if he's around, will get the brunt of the persecution and resulting stress.

Getting Rid of the Shoulds

As Christians, we sometimes impose pressures on ourselves that the Lord would not. We get too wrapped up in what we should do to present a good testimony to the unbelieving world.

We think we should work harder and longer at our jobs than anybody else. We should always have a smile on our face so that a downhearted and discouraged world can see that things are going well for us. We must project that we're on top of it all because we have Jesus.

Some say we should never get angry, yet it is true that bottled up anger or frustration contributes to stress. Anger may sometimes be justified, but it must be tempered with self-control (see Gal. 5:23) and carefully expressed (see Eph. 4:26), or not expressed to other people, but resolved with God alone through prayer. Jesus showed anger and other feelings, including disappointment, discouragement, and loneliness. At other times He entered into joyous celebrations, such as when He contributed to the wedding party by turning water into wine.

Too often Christians try to ignore their feelings, or suppress them—even in their prayers. More than anyone, Jesus could have been caught up in the thinking that He should always be doing His Father's business, but He realized that by living a balanced life He was doing His Father's business. No one knew the depravity of man and his need for a Saviour more than Jesus did, but He was not driven by the lateness of the hour. He knew His own life and ministry would be relatively short. Yet He took time to pray, to fast, to eat, to celebrate, to socialize, to rest, and to meditate. He was faithful to the Father's will.

Too often shoulds are self-imposed—and the reasons for them as well. For example, we should have good marriages, not because we're on center stage and the unbelieving world is watching, but because God ordained the institution and He wants us to enjoy it.

Making Choices

Theological choices and decisions can create stress. When it comes to matters of eternity, we want to make right decisions. Teachings differ on how we come to God and how we are to worship and live. Some say that a person chooses Christ, others that God chooses us in the sacraments. Still others emphasize good works. Views also vary on spiritual gifts and on modes of worship. Charismatic or noncharismatic? Liturgical or not? What about the end times? Are the doomsday preachers right, and if so, should we stock up on candles and dried foods? Political action groups such as Moral Majority want our support. Is their approach valid? What about Christians participating in civil disobedience? We cannot minimize these questions of faith and practice. They require thought—and even study. Their very urgency can be stressful.

Too often we are caught up with trying to do the "right" thing, and trying to please people instead of the Lord. If we concentrated on living to please Him, we would reduce the stress in our lives immeasurably. Our pressure points may never be altered, but *we* will be. We need to get out of the way and let Jesus respond to the stress in our lives. We forget that the Son has made us free, and part of that contract is freedom from stress.

"It is His character that is taken on, but that does not negate the individual's personality. Both the extrovert and the introvert are to be what they are while becoming more like Christ. This does not mean withdrawal or denial of self as much as it does taking on the positive attributes of His love, compassion, and commitment" (James L. Johnson, *How to Enjoy Life and Not Feel Guilty,* Harvest House, p. 35).

It is to the gentle nudge of the Spirit of God to which we must respond and answer. Each of us hears and responds to Him in a different way, because each of us is unique.

I believe that if we seek to live godly, holy lives, tuned to the Spirit of God, we can receive the mind of Christ regarding every stress-producing situation facing us in the 20th century. But we must do our part to maintain a balanced lifestyle—one that includes work, ministry, play, and rest in proper proportions.

Abundant Living

You're a miracle worker, Lord,
   and I'm in the market for one.
You don't have to part the sea for me,
   or send manna from heaven;
But a small-scale miracle
   would restore my faith
   and see me through another week
   crowded with
      decisions
      doubts
      deadlines
      and dilemmas.
A week perhaps light on the victories.
A week not promising the abundant life.

But Father, You came that we might
   have an abundant life.
You came to offer peace,
   even when life lies shattered at our feet,
   in a million little pieces.

Perhaps I've been too caught up
   in a miracle, Lord.
Too caught up with needing a sign.
Perhaps all I really need to do
   is appropriate all of Your
   marvelous promises!

Amen.

4
Lives
Out of Balance

In his book *Prescription for Total Health and Longevity,* Dr. Jonas Miller says, "An automobile mechanic once told me that a car wheel with only a 7-ounce imbalance will produce 13 pounds of imbalance on that wheel when it's spinning at 50 miles per hour. That's like 13 pounds of pressure on the tire at that speed, and it will eventually ruin the ride.

"This is a good example of what happens to you when your life is not in balance . . . the faster you go, the more stress you feel. The bumps of life will take their toll at an earlier age" (Logos International, p. 67).

This was Jane's and my experience: We were "ministry-aholics" and had neglected rest, sleep, relaxation, exercise, leisure, and the good nutrition needed for a balanced life. God knew that 20th-century man would have difficulty maintaining a healthy balance. In His Word we are reminded, "To everything there is a season, and a time to every purpose under heaven" (Ecc. 3:1, KJV). This means there is a time to spend just relaxing. For some this is reading a book or puttering in the flowers. Maybe it is feeling the grass under our feet, the wind at our face, or watching the snow from a fireside chair. If we don't take such time away from daily chores or ministries, we are inviting mental and physical fatigue—and even breakdown.

Trying to Please Everyone

Jane Winn worked in an adult mental health unit of a large Minneapolis hospital. There she encountered Betsy whose psychosis had been triggered by the unbalanced Christian lifestyle. One day Jane was alone with her in the locked unit when suddenly Betsy chased Jane down the hall, knocked her to the floor, and pinned her there for several moments. She began pulling out Jane's hair and continued till help finally arrived.

Fortifying herself with prayer, Jane spent at least an hour a day with the woman, trying to show Christian love to her. Slowly Betsy became involved in some of the activities of the mental health unit and later actually confessed to Jane that she was a Christian, but that she had been so busy being a Christian friend to everyone, saying yes to everyone, accepting projects at her church, and trying to please everybody that her life was out of balance. She allowed no time for rest, relaxation, or family. Guilt crept in, and finally she had a mental breakdown.

As the car wheel spinning out of balance ruins the ride, so we cannot continue indefinitely in an unbalanced lifestyle. Jane's experience working in the mental health unit hammered home to her this important lesson of life.

What do we mean by a balanced life? A look at several definitions of the word *balance* may help us to better understand the concept as it applies to our lives. According to Webster, "balance is the stability produced by an even distribution of weight on each side of the vertical axis." Another definition is "an aesthetically pleasing integration of elements. Harmony." Still another: "Mental and emotional steadiness."

In the following chapters we shall consider the areas of life that are often out of balance, either because of too much emphasis or not enough.

Psalm For A 20TH Century Saint

Call it what you like . . .
  Future shock
  Space-age syndrome
  20th-century trauma . . .
It all adds up to the same thing . . .
We're having a hard time coping, Lord.
The din of my surroundings
  makes Your still, small voice
  more and more difficult to hear.

Perhaps most never listened anyway,
  and so instead they look to the security of
    investments
    tax shelters
    and retirement plans,
  and to the companionship of
    clubs
    encounter groups
    societies
    and campaigns,
  and to the causes of
    peace
    law and order
    and civil rights.
And they've tuned You out, Lord.
They've conveniently shut out
  the One who can restore order and peace
  to 20th-century confusion!

Great God, deal gently with us!
Remind us that we need to turn to You
  much sooner than as a last resort!

Amen.

5
A Balance
of Rest

Rest is not only sleep. It is any time that is not given over to a task or an activity. Rest can be sitting back and thinking about something pleasant. It can be taking a walk or calling a friend. But the attitude must be one of contentment and quiet. We read that God rested after He completed His work of Creation. He probably sat back and enjoyed His handiwork.

We realize the importance of rest when we read "One hand full of rest is better than two fists full of labor" (Ecc. 4:6). Jesus set an example for us too when after the apostles reported to Him what they had done and taught, He said, "Come away by yourselves to a lonely place and rest awhile" (Mark 6:31). The Scripture tells us that so many people had been coming and going, the apostles had had no time to eat.

Needed: Quiet Minds
Admittedly we don't live in a generation that is conducive to peaceful attitudes. But "quiet minds, which are established in stillness, are not perplexed or intimidated. They are like a clock in a thunderstorm, which moves at its own pace" (Tim Hansel, *When I Relax I Feel Guilty,* David C. Cook, p. 22). Clearly only the Prince of Peace can bestow this kind of serenity on us! "Be still and know that I am God" (Ps. 46:10, KJV).

Relaxation, recreation, and leisure, however, are not substitutes for sleep. Sleep is an important aspect of rest and for many people who are tyrannized by stress, it is hard to come by. Most people need seven to eight hours of sleep. God intended for it to be calm and undisturbed sleep (Ecc. 2:23; Ps. 127:2) and the more mental activity we're involved in, the more sleep we need. Peaceful sleep promotes good health, stable emotions, efficient bodies, and even dreams, which are necessary for emotional health.

Too many people, slaves to the time, cut short sleep in order to get everything done. We will accomplish more in the long run if we allow ourselves enough sleep. But again balance is important, for God cautions us: "Do not love sleep, lest you become poor" (Prov. 20:13).

An afternoon nap rejuvenates some people. Winston Churchill took "40 winks" during the day and was refreshed. To fall asleep for a quick nap, however, requires the ability to relax. (More about relaxation techniques later.) I did not have that ability and was a chronic insomniac by age 13. Early in life I had access to sleeping medication, and by the time I was 20 was taking as many as 10 barbiturates a night to relax and fall asleep. The expense was enormous, and I knew it weakened my Christian testimony. As I worked toward a balanced lifestyle, insomnia lessened considerably. Exercising, getting plenty of fresh air, breathing deeply, and practicing various relaxation techniques have reduced my insomnia problem by 90 percent. Cutting down on refined foods and carbohydrates also helped me relax.

Soul Rest
Another aspect of rest is that for the soul. The Bible speaks about a "soul weariness" (Job 10:1) and the antidote for it: "You shall find rest for your souls" (Matt. 11:29). Soul weariness is not new to the 20th century, but it is prevalent in it. It results from deep unrest of the mind and heart and can't be healed by sleep or relaxation. It drains strength and causes insomnia. The world looks for soul rest through such counterfeits as drugs and Eastern meditation, but it is impossible to find it apart from God.

Elijah sat under a juniper tree, tired and depressed after running from the wicked Queen Jezebel. He had traveled by foot many miles in the blazing sun and was in such despair he wanted to die. While he slept, an angel awakened him and gave him nourishment. As his needs were cared for, his emotional problems lifted, and he was able to do what the Lord commanded him (1 Kings 19:4-8). We should not indulge in despair. If we need more physical rest, we should make more time for it. Also, we must *want* a peaceful mind and heart. In Colossians we read, "Let the peace of God rule in your hearts" (3:15, KJV). This implies a letting go of stress, allowing God's peace to take over.

Jesus never promised us a rose garden. But He promised us that in spite of the turmoil of the times, we can have an inner peace; a peace that stems, in part, from a life that includes plenty of sleep and rest.

Uptight World

Are You amused at Your children, Lord?

This week we had another international crisis,
And we turned to the United Nations.

The dollar devaluated again,
And we turned to the Treasury Department.

The unemployment rate went up,
And we turned to Congress.

The stock market plunged,
And we turned to Wall Street
And bought a "how to" book on investments.

Crime and violence went up,
And we endorsed a law and order campaign.

More nations were in turmoil,
And we promoted the Peace Corps.

We've sought all the answers
    from men who have none;
And all they have ever given You
    is a shaking fist.

Father, thank You for Your patience.
Indeed, we deserve these afflictions.
God, reveal Yourself as the only Source
    of refuge
    in a besieged and fractured world,
    and cause us to recognize the futility of
        nuclear disarmament
        United Nations' buffer zones
        high finance and
        international schemes.   Amen.

6
A Balance
of Work

For many people, self-worth is tied up in their work (or ministry). God says our worth should be in Him. But work is highly esteemed in much of society today and many identify themselves in terms of their occupations. Some are never known beyond that facade. Feelings, philosophies, ideas, likes, and dislikes can get lost when we identify ourselves only with our job or ministries.

"Work becomes a measure of our self-worth. To justify our existence and prove to ourselves that we are valuable people, we assume that we must succeed on the job. If we don't succeed at work, so the myth goes, then maybe we aren't worth much. So we start pushing to get ahead, hardly pausing to realize that when one person moves ahead, someone else gets pushed aside" (Dr. Gary Collins, *You Can Profit from Stress,* Vision House, p. 118).

This chapter is not an attack on work, but rather on overwork—the kind that throws our lives dangerously out of balance. God is in favor of work. It was His idea in the first place. "The Lord God took the man and put him in the Garden of Eden to work it and take care of it" (Gen. 2:15, NIV). We also read that "there is nothing better for a man than to eat and drink and tell himself that his labor is good ... that it is from the hand of God"(Ecc. 2:24). It shouldn't be done halfheartedly, but vigorously: "Whatsoever thy hand findeth to do, do it with thy might; for there is no work . . . in the grave" (Ecc. 9:10, KJV).

Importance of Work

Paul, too, stresses the importance of work: "In the name of the Lord Jesus Christ, we command you, brothers, to keep away from every brother who is idle and does not live according to the teaching you received from us. For you yourselves know how you ought to follow our example. We were not idle when we were with you, nor did we eat anyone's food without paying for it. On the contrary; we worked night and day, laboring and toiling so that we would not be a burden to any of you. We did this, not because we do not have the right to such help, but in order to make ourselves a model for you to follow. For even when we were with you, we gave you this rule: 'If a man will not work, he shall not eat'" (2 Thes. 3:6-10, NIV). In 1 Timothy we read that those who will not work and provide for their own are "worse than infidels" (5:8, KJV).

We know that Paul helped earn his living as a tentmaker. David was a shepherd, and Jesus was a carpenter. So if God originated the idea of working, where did we go wrong?

When God made Adam and gave him dominion over creation, He intended work to be an opportunity for man to use his creative abilities and reflect God's glory. But after the Fall, work too often became a means of exalting self rather than exalting God. It became an end in itself. A "workaholic" or a "ministry-aholic" can hardly glorify God; he may actually drive people away from the kingdom of God.

We are cautioned to keep the right perspective on our work. First, we must recognize God in it or we become vain and view it as our accomplishment (Ecc. 2:4-11). We are to put our hearts into our work as though we are working for the Lord, for we are! "It is the Lord Christ you are serving" (Col. 3:23-24, NIV).

The Bible also warns us not to let the riches of work tempt us too greatly. "There was no end to all his labor. Indeed, his eyes were not satisfied with riches and he never asked, 'For whom am I laboring and depriving myself of pleasure?'" (Ecc. 4:8) In Proverbs we read, "Do not weary yourself to gain wealth; cease from your consideration of it. When you set your eyes on it, it is gone" (23:4-5). Some people do little but work to get wealth and when they achieve it are too worn out or sick to enjoy it. Or they spend it recklessly and it is gone before they know it.

Satisfaction or Stress?

Work should bring us satisfaction and other good things. "He that tilleth his land shall be satisfied with bread" (Prov. 12:11). For those of us who aren't farmers, work assures us of having money for buying food. Since work is a gift from God, we must enjoy it and not let it become a vanity (Ecc. 2:11).

Work is clearly one of the chief producers of stress, and much job-related stress is uncontrollable. Work stress has intensified the last 25 years. In the fierce competition of the last two decades, pressure begins at the top of the ladder and works its way down. Quotas are upped, territories expanded, and more is demanded of employees at every level. Expectations constantly increase. There's not much abiding in business.

We hear a lot about job burnout. Prison guards often succumb to stress in less than 10 years. The high rate of alcoholism among police officers indicates their job stress is high. Firemen, waitresses, and secretaries are also singled out. Teachers too are prime candidates for job burnout with 100,000 a year assaulted by students.

A person experiencing job burnout will be more prone to utilize escape tactics such as excessive drinking or eating, or wanting to stay in bed. He will have little enthusiasm for his job, his inefficiency increases, and he will be extremely tired after work. The burnout victim may have various aches and pains, chronic stiff neck or a back problem, insomnia, and even suffer chronic alcoholism, depression, or bleeding ulcers. By that time, the job controls the burnout victim.

This problem is getting so acute that many companies are investing millions of dollars to protect their employees. Some give a 3-month paid leave of absence after 10 years of service. Exercise and aerobic dance courses are being made available for employees during the lunch hour (see chapter 8). Some companies insist that employees get away from their desk at midday. Others are investing in sports and health equipment or providing jogging trails, tennis courts, softball fields, and swimming pools on the company grounds.

Some companies now realize that our bio-rhythms are thrown off when we must work varying shifts—that the body doesn't function well when coping with inconsistent routines—and they operate only two workshifts instead of three.

Job burnout knows no economic status. The assembly-line worker must deal with the stress of boredom, the busy executive with the stress of heavy responsibilities, red tape, and bureaucracy.

Women Have Special Frustrations

Burnout is not limited to men. Skyrocketing inflation and the cost of homes have forced back to work some women who would prefer to be home raising a family. A woman may be assigned a more "lowly" job because she is not "the head of the home." She also can be the brunt of jokes and sexual harrassment on the job. Even if she is as qualified as a man, she may never advance very high up the ladder.

The working mother is often concerned that she is unable to spend enough quality time with her children. Unless her job is one she especially wanted, it may not provide the satisfaction she could get in the home, and this can leave her frustrated and angry. Further, unless family members help, her home and job duties make the possibility of a balanced lifestyle remote. Meals may not be as carefully planned and nutritious, family togetherness breaks down, and the only exercise she gets is when she unloads the washing machine.

And yet millions of American women thrive on this type of pace. I have a friend who has won the "Consultant of the Year" award in the employment business four times and each time in a period of a depressed economy when businesses were cutting back on their hiring. When she started in the business in the early 1970s, she was making $575 a month. Now she makes eight times that amount. She admits that she easily gets caught up in the competitive drive to make the most of job placements. Everybody likes to win—even Christians!

She has to work at not letting her job run her life. To get her mind off of herself, her quotas, her placements, and her potential first-place trips to Hawaii, she shows concern for other people. She is an encourager and a good listener. She goes to lunch with friends who are not associated with her job, draws them out, and focuses on them.

Being so other-directed has impressed her work associates, most of whom are not Christians. Following an acceptance speech she gave as "Consultant of the Year," she received a standing ovation. Her life stacked up with the message of her speech.

Myths About Work

In his book, Tim Hansel points out nine notions about work that we should be wary of:

- Work is our primary source of identity.
- Work is inherently good, and therefore, the more you do, the better person you are.
- You are not really serving the Lord unless you consistently push to the point of fatigue.
- The more you work, the more God loves you.
- If you work hard enough 50 weeks a year, then you "deserve" a 2-week vacation.
- The purpose of work is to make enough money to buy things so you can be happy.
- Most of your problems would be solved if you would only work harder.
- The Bible says that the most important thing a person can do is work.
- The biggest problem in our society is that people don't work hard enough (*When I Relax I Feel Guilty*, David C. Cook, p. 37).

I was guilty of embracing many of these ideas. Time away from work or ministry was "wasted time." When people challenged my total preoccupation, I became defensive. I was a classic case of both "workaholic" and "ministry-aholic." I answered yes to the following tests of a workaholic:

Are You a Workaholic?

Check *Yes* or *No* and find out.

	Yes	No
Do you WORK nearly every day?		
Do you often WORK more than you really enjoy?		

Do you WORK more than most of your associates?
Do you sometimes WORK alone and in secret?
Does WORKing help you forget some of your problems?
Do you feel more self-confident and sociable when you WORK?
Do you sometimes excuse yourself from other activities in order to WORK?
Has your health suffered because you WORK too much?
Does WORKing sometimes make you moody and depressed?
Do you WORK more now than when you were younger?
Has WORKing interfered with your family or community responsibilities?
Do you sometimes brag about how much you WORK?
Do you resent people who do not like to WORK?
Has WORKing become the center of your lifestyle?
Do you get restless when you have not been WORKing for several days?
Are you angry if someone questions or criticizes your WORKing habits?
Would you feel lost and afraid if you had to stop WORKing?
Do you envy those who are able to WORK more than you do?
Have you ever felt that you could do more with your life if you gave up WORKing?
Do questions like these about WORK make you angry?
(Gordon J. Dahl, Leisure Education Resources)

Words for a Workaholic
This was written for people like the author.

If I work with the strength of men and machines, but have not leisure, I am a noisy brute or a clumsy clod. And if I have skills for complex technology, or powers to move mountains of bureaucracy, or knowledge to understand great problems, but have not leisure, I am nothing. If I give of myself to everyone, and if I sacrifice my own bodily needs for the sake of my job, but have no leisure, I gain nothing.

Leisure is found in being patient and kind; it is not in striving or competing or conquering. Leisure does not insist upon progress or success. It is not angry when someone fails, nor resentful when someone else does better. Leisure is not fully experienced when we are able to bear all things, believe all things, hope all things, and enjoy all things.

Leisure never ends. As for our work, it will pass away. As for our skills and powers, they will cease. As for our knowledge, it will fade away. For our knowledge is imperfect and our work imperfect; but when the perfect life comes, our imperfections will all disappear.

When I was a slave, I worked like a slave, I spoke like a slave, I thought like a slave; but when I became a free person, I gave up slavish ways (Gordon J. Dahl, Leisure Education Resources).

The workaholic is out of balance as much as the perennial parasite on welfare. The workaholic may think he is "saving humanity" with an 80-hour workweek; but he may be ignoring his family and other responsibilities. Chances are his motive for helping humanity is borne out of a strong need for approval. He probably feels like a nobody, so works to prove that he is a somebody. If he can attain power, position, or prestige, he can prove to the world, and more importantly, perhaps, to himself, that he has worth.

The workaholic is always planning for the future—never satisfied with the present. He is driven, but driven from *within*.

Daniel Had a Secular Job

Some people assume that those in full-time Christian work have been "called" while those in secular work have not. This suggests that the Christian worker is of greater usefulness to God. God is in favor of secular work! Daniel was assigned to secular duties in Babylon. There was little there that appealed to him, but he worked right in the middle of Bablyon's corruption. Separation from the world took place only in his heart, but that was acceptable to God. Daniel made no attempt to remove himself from his assignment. Instead he "made up his mind that he would not defile himself" (Dan. 1:8). Babylon and all it represents is abominable in God's sight, yet God dared to send Daniel into the midst of it.

Working in the secular realm is not an easy assignment. Christians must tolerate gossip, cheating, lying, phony smiles, selfish ambition, and an intense love of money.

"As the Father has sent Me, I also send you" (John 20:21). This is a mandate to go into the world. Many Christians want only the bliss of a Christian community and can hardly wait for heaven. Paul said that if staying here [in the world] would benefit people, he would stay even though he wanted to go to be with Christ (Phil. 1:23).

By our daily experiences on the secular job, we may actually influence as many people for God as those who serve in full-time service. We are in the world to be lights and salt. The secular field is fertile. People are often successful and yet, like Solomon, "all is vanity" to them. They may have power, money, and success, but no peace or contentment. They are ready to have someone tell them that there is a better way.

God wants to establish His kingdom in the business world where there are men and women who are disciplined, who know how to follow orders and how to deal with people. These are tremendous attributes when such people become Christians.

The Lord calls some from secular jobs into the ministry, but most Christians are in secular work. We are to be useful to God right where we are; to bloom where we are planted.

Making Work an Idol

"Yes, work is both good and necessary. It should be pursued with diligence, honesty, and pride. But it should not be worshiped and glorified as the basis of human dignity and worth. People are valuable apart from their job productivity. Work never saved anyone from sin, death, or evil; nor has it ever unilaterally produced faith, hope, and love. When work becomes a person's all-consuming interest, even if the work is good and necessary, it is idolatry" (Hansel, *When I Relax,* p. 35).

Though work is good, it should never get in the way of our

salvation or keep us too preoccupied to hear the voice of the Lord.

The early Christians put primary emphasis on total Christian living, rather than on their jobs. Their priority was the abundant Christian life and the fulfillment of God's will for their lives. They weren't all that concerned about budgets, deadlines, and overtime. Success and ambition weren't as important because their worth wasn't tied up with it. Their worth came from a relationship with God.

"To be really successful in God's eyes our lives must be characterized by *holiness.* 'I urge you therefore, brethren, by the mercies of God, to present your bodies a living and *holy* sacrifice acceptable to God' (Rom. 12:1). This is not a popular idea. We live in a time when getting ahead in one's work is considered far more important than living a holy life which is acceptable to God. It seems to me, however, that we could reach the height of success in terms of money, prestige, promotions, and acclaims; we could be successful leaders—even Christian leaders—but still be failures in God's sight because we neglect true holiness. Too often we are so busy getting ahead with our work that there is no time for prayer, meditation, or thoughts about holy living" (Collins, *You Can Profit,* p. 121).

In contrast, Tim Hansel paints a poignant picture of Jesus, our example: "I don't understand how the Master could take time to go alone into the desert to fast and pray when the whole world was starving and in chaos, when countless individuals needed Him. He had a proven track record of healing. I just don't understand . . . but He did. I don't understand how He would continue to love and give when He was rejected like He was. And how He could respond rather than react. And how He could maintain His inner poise rather than project pain.

"I don't understand how He could tell us not to worry about life when times are so difficult (Luke 12:22). I don't know how He could tell us that some of us are working too hard . . . that we're too busy, and that our busyness will actually cause us to miss the kingdom of God (Luke 14:16-24).

"I don't understand how He could say that sometimes it is better to sit at His feet than to be up doing things for Him (Luke 10:38-42). Or how He could promise rest in the midst of a world filled with turmoil and distorted with pain (Matt. 11:28-30). Or how He could ask us to be like little children, when the world needs more firm leadership and harder workers. I don't understand how Jesus could play and celebrate and enjoy life, when the world was in the condition it was in (Matt. 11:19).

"I don't understand . . . but he did" (Hansel, *When I Relax*, p. 59).

Hard work rarely hurts anyone, but the *stress* associated with *overwork* in your job or ministry is destructive. The person who works hard must be sure to play hard.

7
A Balance
of Recreation

Workaholics and ministry-aholics know very little about leisure or recreation. Words like fun, play, and amusement are foreign to them.

With the trend toward a shorter workweek, middle-class Americans have more leisure time. Yet some are uncomfortable about that, feeling guilty if they "fritter time away." The leisure revolution runs counter to what we have been taught is ethical. Many feel leisure is not worth the same "hourly rate" as work or ministry time.

I wrongly believed that leisure implies laziness, too much comfort, and a self-indulgent way of life, that it is wasted time. I viewed leisure as "unchristian"—almost immoral and wondered how a Christian can indulge in leisure in light of the tragedy and chaos in the world.

Time: Tyrant or Friend?
Tim Hansel responds to this type of thinking in his book *When I Relax I Feel Guilty.* "In our worthy attempt to avoid idleness and questionable pleasures, we begin to feel that everything must be useful. Thus our false guilt compels us to read for profit, attend parties for contacts, exercise so we can work better, and rest in order to be more efficient. We regress to a kind of neopuritanism that says, 'You have not been born into the world for pleasure.' A curious and familiar psychological need to justify everything emerges, leaving no room for discovery and pure enjoyment.

"Time becomes a tyrant instead of a friend. Joy becomes something we will do later. Play becomes something for children. Creativity becomes the unattainable quality of artists and poets instead of the essence of our lives. Wonder is just the name of a bread, and imagination doesn't make enough money to be worthwhile" (p. 12).

An unknown author expresses the results of a "wasted hour."

I wasted an hour one morning beside a mountain stream,
I seized a cloud from the sky above, and fashioned myself a dream;
In the hush of the early twilight, far from the haunts of men,
I wasted a summer evening, and fashioned my dream again.
Wasted? Perhaps.
Folks say so who never have walked with God,
When lanes are purple with lilacs or yellow with goldenrod.
But I have found strength for my labors in that one short evening hour,
I have found joy and contentment; I have found peace and power.
My dreaming has left me a treasure, a hope that is strong and true,
From wasted hours I have built my life, and found my faith anew.

We need to learn a basic principle of stress reduction: If we work hard, we must play hard. Our play can take many forms: We can watch a sunset, walk in the woods, read, listen to music, or talk to a friend. We can feed the birds, stroll through a museum, or go to a ball game. We can sit in the sun, learn to play an instrument, or take up a hobby.

Leisure is not a luxury; it is a *necessity*. It can make our days count, rather than we counting our days. Leisure may not always be of spiritual significance, but it provides a necessary change of pace. Perhaps we need to be more creative in our pursuit of leisure. Some entertainment is too expensive, some is inappropriate for a believer, but too often eating becomes our leisure activity.

Leisure activities need not be exotic, or expensive, or warrant tons of gear. Though Madison Avenue tries to convince us that we must spend lots of money on leisure to enjoy it, many outdoor activities are still free.

Too often we save for a vacation, and assume leisure is only a once-a-year thing. We go all-out to make it exotic. We put ourselves under stress getting ready for it and then cramming everything into the time we have. We *work at our leisure* as well as at our work! It may be beneficial to consider more frequent mini-vacations. More frequent changes of scenery renew our vitality and ease our stress if they are in restful environments. We should never take work-related problems on vacations!

Tips for Quiet Leisure

If you're having trouble allowing for leisure or knowing how to spend it consider these suggestions:

• Plan your leisure time well in advance and protect it in the same way you protect the time allotted for your job. Refuse to accept responsibilities that might interfere with leisure pursuits.

• Try loafing now and then. Or just listening to the birds, the wind, or the rain. Try gazing at the clouds as you stretch out on a lawn chair or swing in a hammock.

• Develop a hobby. It should be a hobby that is on-going, though it may have completion aspects to it. It should be one you can pick up and lay down at any time. Make sure you use different muscles and positions than you do at work. It should not be too expensive, for that will bring on added stress. Decide if you have enough ability for the hobby. If not, can you develop it? Will it cause friction in your family? Will it take too much time and require more energy than you have?

• Develop a *group* interest. Groups provide the climate for social interaction. You might join an ethnic dancing group, if that is an interest, or a group that attends the theatre, or musical events. Hobby clubs offer opportunities for people to share in like interests.

• Find a sport in which you can participate and practice at least once a week. There's hiking, tennis, racquetball, handball, bowling, fishing, swimming, softball, skiing, jogging, or even walking. But don't undertake too many of these. Resist the urge to go sailing and fishing during the day and bowling and jogging at night. Spread it out!

• Become a member of a social group—a small circle of friends that gets together regularly for fellowship and recreation. Churches often offer opportunities for a sense of belonging and, at the same time, are helping to further the work of the Lord.

- Enjoy giving of yourself. How about volunteer work?
- Plan regular times away from home. Then don't do anything that is job-related. Don't call your office to see how things are going. Don't race home to return your phone calls.
- Explore something you feel you might like to do but always have been afraid to try. Plunge in and give it your best.

Gordon Dahl also suggests: "Take a leisure resources inventory. Make a list of the schools, libraries, and other places where you can take classes and learn more about things that interest you. Make a list of achievements or goals, of persons you enjoy being with, of friends or relatives you would like to visit, of places you would like to go and programs in which you would like to participate. You might make a list of books you want to read, movies and plays you want to see, and concerts you want to attend; of things you enjoy doing for other people, of people for whom you would like to do something special, and some talents or skills you have that you want to offer to anyone in need" *(Leisure Education Resources).*

Leisure needs to be seen as a service to others, not just as the opposite of work. Leisure can revitalize our inner being and allow our faith to be more robust. Then we can be more effective witnesses.

We never will know our true capabilities unless we take time to explore them and then settle on a healthy balance of work and leisure. God made us human, so we needn't try to transcend that. Our witness is more effective when the world sees us participating in normal, everyday activities.

God is not a referee with a stop watch, making sure we use every second for His kingdom. He wants us to take time to enjoy the world He created for us. He wants us to have an abundant life that includes opportunities for wholesome recreation. Leisure is God's time as much as the time we spend in ministry or work.

The world is not impressed with one who is a slave to work or ministry. In order for us to be effective witnesses, people need to see us enjoying free time in wholesome, creative ways.

Leisure gives us time to pause, to reflect, to contemplate, and to search. Our minds become less cluttered and we are better able to hear God speak to us.

The truly full life is a rhythm of work and leisure.

8
A Balance
of Exercise

Technology has been hard on the human body. The body improves when it is exercised, and most human bodies are clamoring to be used. In America, many would not pass a basic fitness test.

Rudyard Kipling once said, "Nations have passed away and left no trace. History gives the cause of this; one single, simple reason in all cases; they fell because their people were not fit."

Tests have shown that twice as many sedentary persons as active ones have heart attacks. Most ulcer and diabetes sufferers are inactive people. Less active people also are more susceptible to emotional difficulties. Though exercise is hailed as the natural tranquilizer, we say, "Who wants to work up a sweat in an air-conditioned society?" Instead many try to fight stress with alcohol or tranquilizers. More than $100 million is spent on tranquilizers each year and alcohol abuse is rampant.

When one doctor recommended exercise for my serious stress problem, it seemed absurd because I was already so tired I could hardly function. I had no time to relax or rest, much less exercise. I eyed his prescription pad and hoped he would write out a prescription for a pill that would more conveniently dispose of my symptoms. But he chose not to be another "poison-peddler." Rather, he recommended a generous daily dose of the only "safe tranquilizer" he knows and that is exercise. I shall forever be grateful.

God wants us to glorify Him in our bodies: "Your body is the temple of the Holy Spirit . . . therefore glorify God in your body" (1 Cor. 6:19-20). There is nothing God-honoring about flabby, sick, out-of-breath Christians!

Fortunately, some encouraging signs are showing up. "Between 1968 and 1978 there were actually 21 percent fewer deaths from heart attacks. . . . And the only major thing that has changed in the health habits of the American people has been their increased interest in exercise" (Dr. Kenneth Cooper, "The Healthy Christian," *New Wine* magazine, April '79, p. 5). In 1968 it was estimated there were fewer than 100,000 jogging. A decade later, estimates were as high as 25 million. Brisk walking may be as popular as jogging.

Aerobic Exercises Gain Popularity

Dr. Kenneth Cooper has revolutionized exercise with his aerobic concept. Aerobic exercise is not designed for muscle building or figure shaping, but for cardiovascular-pulmonary conditioning . . . building an endurance base in the heart, blood vessels, and lungs. In the process it decreases triglycerides and cholesterol levels in the blood. It also decreases hormone production, which is good because too much adrenaline can cause problems in the arteries.

Aerobic exercisers unanimously report quieted emotions and untroubled sleep. Their lungs are developed, which gets more oxygen into the blood stream. Blood pressure is usually lowered and less acid is produced in the stomach, because pent-up aggression is released through exercise. Joggers admit that if for some reason they stop the activity, they lose their enthusiasm for life and feeling of well-being, and also notice a reduction in their productivity. Popular aerobic exercises include running, swimming, biking, tennis, cross-country skiing, racquetball, and brisk walking. All demand plenty of oxygen.

Dr. Cooper is the director of the Aerobics Center in Dallas. He is a Christian and has done extensive research on the benefits of exercise. In an interview in *New Wine* magazine, he says: "I feel that we are commanded to take care of our bodies as well as our spirits. . . . I think that at times we as Christians tend to negate this aspect of the commandment we have been given. As a result, we are very likely to suffer from obesity, inactivity, and from a lack of optimum productivity.

"In other words, we haven't built the structure or foundation by which to propagate the Good News as we might if we were physically fit. . . . I have tried to motivate Christians to be concerned not only about spiritual things but also physical. I have seen Christians so heavenly oriented, they forget what they are doing on earth" ("The Healthy Christian," p. 5).

Aerobic exercises require some of the vigor, vitality, speed, endurance, and stamina of youth. In addition to aerobic exercises, there are stretching and bending exercises which restore more elasticity to joints and muscles, and progressive resistance exercises, such as training with weights. These restore firm muscle tone and the symmetrical athletic build.

If we stick with only one form of exercise, such as jogging, we will receive the benefits of only that type of exercise. Since no single type provides all benefits the body needs, it is good to set up a program that will include a variety.

It took awhile for me to act on the exercise advice given me. It was suggested that I take a simple test to determine what kind of shape I was in. I pressed my finger against the carotid artery in the side of my neck and checked the beat of the pulse against a sweep second hand for 60 seconds. I was told that if the beat at rest is 80 or more a minute, one is *not* in good condition. Less than 60 is considered excellent, and 70 is average. My pulse consistently beat 95 times a minute or more. I got the message.

Jane Winn realized the value of exercise earlier than I did. She saw it greatly reduce stress-related problems in her life, and it particularly improved her sleep. She realized the importance of exercise even more strongly when she served as a recreational therapist in a major Minneapolis hospital. Her depressed patients had pale complexions, little ability to concentrate, and no motivation. Because of their inactivity, very little oxygen was released to their brains. This inactivity heightened their symptoms.

After she initiated an exercise program for them, she noticed immediate improvement. Their depression, anger, and even psychotic behavior lessened. It was not easy to get them involved in the program, but once they were, the patients noted improvement in themselves. They reported sleeping better, having more energy and confidence, and not wanting so much junk food.

Lunch-Break Exercise Programs
With such dramatic response, Jane took her idea into the business world and formed Caspian Associates. It is a simple program designed for people in business and industry. It is a basic exercise program combining dance steps with stretching exercises and music. The exercises coincide with the exact beat of the music. The program fits well in a 15-minute coffee break or a lunch break.

Stress-ridden employees have told her, "I no longer get drowsy in the afternoon" or they say, "After a brief workout, the fog clears, and I've still got energy when I get home."

A spokesman for one of the largest corporations in the Minneapolis area told her, "If your program can help even one employee in preventing a heart attack or other stress-related illness, it will be more than worth it for us."

This interest in the fitness of employees is growing. Industry is finding that company-sponsored fitness programs are reducing absenteeism, accidents, and sick pay. Their employees are more alert and productive, and morale is higher. Whatever money firms must invest in these programs comes back to them in terms of healthier more efficient employees.

Plan Your Own Program
Here are tips to help you plan your own exercise program:
 • Start today while you still feel good. Don't wait until you have chest pains or dizziness because of high blood pressure.
 • Train, don't strain. Don't overdo in your enthusiasm. It will only discourage you if you push too hard. The line that says you're not accomplishing anything unless it hurts is not true. People often feel that if some is good, more is better, and go overboard.
 • In jogging, set your own pace. It doesn't have to be painful. Slow down to a brisk walk if you get winded and when you recover, start

jogging again. Increase distance and pace gradually by working at it at least three times a week. Keep in mind long, slow, distance. Be sure to invest in a pair of good jogging shoes and avoid running on concrete as much as possible. For safety choose clothing colors that can be easily seen.

• If you begin a walking program, don't saunter. Rather, proceed at a vigorous pace, head up, chest out, and arms swinging freely. A daily walk can work wonders in restoring youthful health and vigor. Wear well-cushioned jogging shoes and use a long stride. The next time your friends ask you to a coffee party, try to sell them on a 30-minute walk instead. But remember, this is one occasion when you don't take time to smell the flowers!

• Find an exercise activity that is *fun*. If it is not enjoyable, the program will be primarily guilt-induced—something you should do—and you will put it off. Practice it several times a week. For variety select two or three activities and intersperse them throughout the week. Consider the cost involved, and the convenience factor. Check into local activities at the YMCA as well as local park board and school adult education programs. Keep travel time to a minimum.

• Get some form of exercise each day. Make it a habit. If you find yourself short of time for this new project, then *make time*. It is a matter of priority. If you want something—such as good health—badly enough, you will earmark time. It is amazing how much time heart attack victims budget for their daily exercise! Don't wait until it is a case of have-to.

• In addition to a daily exercise of 15 minutes, try to work in a one-hour aerobic exercise at least three times a week.

• Don't be discouraged if results aren't noticeable immediately. Within a month, however, you should see and feel signs of great improvement. You may feel more productive and more vigorous. You may have shifted some weight and even lost a few pounds. Generally, you'll feel more healthy.

• Listen to your body. When it says stop, stop! Remember, too much exercise can be as dangerous as too little exercise, so again *balance* is the key word.

Calculating a Stress Quotient

The amount of exercise each of us should get varies, because our endurance limits are not the same. Our oxygen intake varies, as does our metabolic rate. But if we're in normal health, our pulse will indicate immediately whether or not we are exercising within safe limits. To calculate your own stress quotient, subtract your age (say 59) from 220. The answer is 161 beats per minute (bpm), the maximum possible heart rate for a person aged 59.

If you are between ages 30 and 55, a quick way to tell if you are overdoing is to rest for exactly one minute after exercising and then take your pulse. If it registers over 130 bpm, reduce your pace and distance till your pulse registers closer to 100. If after resting five minutes your pulse registers over 120, this is a definite sign of fatigue. If after resting for 10 minutes, your pulse registers over 100, this confirms that you are pushing yourself too hard. These figures should be gradually reduced for those over 55. Always stay within safe limits as you increase your pace and distance.

It is wise to check with your doctor before launching an exercise program. This is particularly true if you are over 35 and unable to walk a mile in 18 minutes, if you are obese, are a heavy smoker or drinker, are on medication, or have high blood pressure or cardiovascular problems. Your doctor can give you a stress EKG test to reveal your maximum safe heartbeat rate and any valid reason why you should not exercise.

Final advice: Your more active life is going to require a complete nutritional base. You will have to eat right and supplement your diet with vitamins. Vigorous exercises create special demands for the water-soluble B-complex and C vitamins which must be replaced daily. Vitamin E and an adequate supply of iron, calcium, magnesium, and potassium are also essential. These nutrients play a role in transporting oxygen through the bloodstream to rejuvenate and repair aging cells and tissue. Calcium, magnesium, and potassium also build bones and help prevent muscle cramps. See more on nutrition and vitamins in chapter 10.

Jane and I have found that exercise is imperative in battling stress and such allies as depression, fatigue, irritability, and insomnia. An hour of exercise chases away the "blues" and relaxes me to where sleeping medication is nearly a thing of the past. The more I exercise, the more my appetite is *decreased*. I desire less junk food and sugar. I am less tense and anxious, and more fun to be around.

Exercise ranks high as a stress reducer, and as a "cure" for a multitude of ills. Give it a try!

9
A Balance
of Relaxation

A common misconception is that rest and relaxation are the same. Not so!

Rest may take the form of reading, chatting with a friend, or even taking a nap. *Relaxation* requires a conscious effort; it is a learned technique. We must practice it faithfully in order to achieve maximum results. By tensing and relaxing various muscle groups in our bodies, we can learn to lower the level of stress.

The goal of the various relaxation techniques is to slow down the body's rapid response rate. When we are relaxed, our breathing becomes deep and slow; the heart rate decreases and the blood flow to the hands and feet increases. Muscles relax and hormonal equilibrium is established; metabolism is generally slowed.

Medical experts tell us that most people use about 30 percent of their total lung capacity. Breathing deeply during periods of relaxation drives air into the bottom of our lungs. Stress experts agree that even 20 minutes of relaxation and deep breathing a day will vastly improve physical health and emotional stability. The deep breathing sends a surge of oxygen-charged blood to the surface of the skin and improves color.

The breathing exercises can be done throughout the day. Next time you want to grind your teeth in a traffic jam or a grocery line, or feel like laying on your horn, take a deep breath instead. Do this often. The key to relaxation is a quiet environment, a passive attitude, and a comfortable position. So find a spot in your house where you can unwind. It may be a "prayer closet" or a comfortable chair. When you retreat to it, don't think about the cares of the day, but don't blank out your mind either.

"If you put worrisome [stressful] thoughts out of your mind but do not replace them with something positive, you will probably revert to the negative pattern of thinking. Your mind cannot be blank. If you don't fill it with something positive, it will go back to the negative because it knows that the best" (Norman Wright, *An Answer to Worry and Anxiety,* Harvest House, p. 52).

Jesus told the story of the man who had been delivered of a demon, but the demon found seven other unclean spirits and entered the man again because his heart was empty (Matt. 12:43-45). Clear your mind of the cares of the day and focus on the goodness of the Lord, a pleasant event in life, or a relaxing situation.

Some may suggest meditating, but we must be cautious. Meditating on Jesus is one thing, but yoga and Transcendental Meditation are based on a mystical philosophy and it is impossible to practice either without being caught up in those overtones. "TM is a particular snare today because there are tests that show that blood pressure drops and breathing and heartbeat slows when one is practicing it" (Dr. Gary Collins, *You Can Profit from Stress,* Vision House, p. 194). Advocates of TM will insist that it is based strictly on scientific technique and that it is not a religious movement. But consider the *mantra* ("Hindu Sanskrit incantation") that the meditator is to repeat over and over. "Maharishi Mahesh Yogi, the TM seer, says, 'we do something . . . according to Vedic rites, particularly chanting to produce an effect in some other world, and draw the attention of those higher beings or gods living there'" (Collins, *You Can Profit,* p. 194). We are told to "resist the devil" (James 4:7). Blanking out our minds or chanting may open us up to demonic influences.

Practice Relaxation Techniques
It is good to set aside a certain time and place to practice relaxation

techniques. Finding a spot where you are least likely to be disturbed is best. You might want to take the telephone off the hook. Plan on 15 to 20 minutes, no matter how busy the day. Ideally this should be done twice a day; once in the morning and before retiring.

Sit or lie, and purposely tense up some of the muscles in your body. First one arm, then the other. One leg, then the other. Tense them for several seconds—till you feel that you are straining. Then relax the muscles and notice the surge of relaxation that comes into them. As you focus on this good feeling, you will lessen overall tension. At the same time note your sense of calmness and serenity, and your freedom from stress. Don't listen to sounds around you, only to your breathing. This is one occasion when you think only about yourself.

Tense your right foot as if to squeeze out all the tensions; then let go. Do the same with the left foot, but keep the rest of the body loose as you tense each part. Tense, then relax, the shoulders and neck.

Bend slowly to the right, taking time to lower the head as far as it will go; then slowly bend to the left as far down as you can go and slowly straighten up. Exercise such facial muscles as eyelids, cheekbones, and the jaw. Consider other areas of your body and concentrate on them: the hips, waist, rib cage, spine, fingers, and toes. You will feel your body "letting go." Your breathing may slow down so that you hardly notice it. Be aware of how quiet you can be. Sense the tension leaving your body as you concentrate on it. Learn that you can bring your body to a relaxed state whenever you choose. You can control your body—it doesn't have to control you. (There are times when it is appropriate to be wound up, but the trick is to be able to choose.)

At one time Jane and I were convinced that insomnia was to be our "thorn in the flesh." We tried various methods to get relief and all we had to show for it was a high pharmacy bill. We even arranged our job/ministry so that we could sleep in, knowing that sleep often eluded us till 2 or 3 A.M. We memorized all the verses on sleep in the Bible, but we didn't realize that God wanted us to do our part, and that meant changing our lifestyles.

When we faithfully practice our relaxation exercises a half hour a day, sleep disturbances are under control. Tension headaches and stiff necks also ease. It may sound simple, too simple for you to believe. Twenty minutes of quality relaxation time a day will make you more efficient and much easier to get along with!

I urge you to learn from my mistakes. Start practicing a relaxation technique today—even if you think you don't need it. It is better to learn the skill before you're under great stress. By the time I realized my need to work on relaxation, I was so frazzled and stress-filled I couldn't clear my mind. As a result I had to train my body to relax through biofeedback.

Monitoring Our Bodies

With today's delicate electronic devices we can know what is going on within our bodies. It was once thought that we could never consciously control our pulse rates and oxygen consumption. Then animal tests showed us we can. Monitoring devices attached to us can actually feed back to us such bodily processes as heartbeat or brain waves. In my case, a beep measured stress and tension. The greater the stress, the faster the beep would go—and on me it frequently sounded like a Geiger counter!

By practicing relaxation exercises throughout the week, I could eventually alter the rate of the beep significantly. I learned how to relax. It took several months and was expensive, but finally that little beep was brought down close to the normal range and I realized that I finally was able to control the stress in my life. It was becoming a natural function to relax my body when I wanted to.

Since some relaxation techniques can alter body-regulation, you may want to discuss the program with your doctor. As a result of increased relaxation, repressed feelings may surface and be released, but so will your anxiety and fear surrounding them.

It is unfortunate that our generation can no longer respond normally to stress and tension; that technology has had to devise machines to assist us in the job; that most people's definition of relaxation is the Indianapolis 500 or a movie. We can be thankful God gives insight to stress experts who have devised simple and inexpensive relaxation exercises. But like anything, if we want to be good at relaxing, we've got to practice.

10
A Balance
of Nutrition

It's been estimated that America's food consumption is double what it should be. Christians probably sin most often against their bodies by eating too many calories and the wrong kinds of foods.

God wants us to "be in health, even as thy soul prospereth" (3 John 2, KJV). The old saying is still true: we are what we eat; and many people are digging their graves with their teeth.

When we eat the wrong foods, we counteract much of the good we are doing to combat stress in other areas of our lives.

Stress results from eating certain foods which cause bodily functions to be adversely influenced. Since stress is the response of the body to any demand made on it, certain foods cause the body to focus attention on them because they are in some way harmful.

For example, take a piece of pie. When we eat it, our blood sugar rises dramatically. Our bodies must respond to this rise in blood sugar by having the pancreas pump out insulin to drive the blood sugar down. The adrenal glands then attempt to stabilize the blood sugar by pouring out adrenal hormones. Over the years, the body loses its ability to repair efficiently and it begins to break down.

It is believed that there were fewer heart attacks 50 years ago not only because there was less stress, but because sugar and refined foods were not as abundant then, and evidence shows that the nations with the highest incidence of heart problems are ones that consume the most sugar.

If you think you can endure 20th-century stress on a diet of coffee, carbohydrates, and sugar, you're headed for a crash. If you're denying yourself a balanced diet, which should be high in protein, minerals, and vitamins, you're going to relegate yourself to a lowered intellectual level and a tired, stress-ridden state.

"Your body is made to be operated by food. It's made out of nutrients and must be replenished—as the Lord made so clear when He raised the young girl from the dead (Mark 5:39-43). The last thing He said to the people after He had brought the girl back to life was 'something should be given her to eat'" (Dr. Jonas Miller, *Prescription for Total Health and Longevity,* Logos, p. 77).

Today families seldom eat breakfast together; rarely do they have lunch at home. We're eating wherever we happen to be, and often that's at a fast-food restaurant. Studies have shown that many essential nutrients are missing from these foods which, in addition to being poor nutritionally, are loaded with salt, carbohydrates, and calories. The price might be right, but we are being shortchanged in other respects.

Dr. Brian Briggs is a Christian physician who treats his patients with Orthomolecular Medicine—diet, nutrition, vitamins, and minerals. Some look on his methods as innovative and somewhat controversial. The fact that he prays for his patients, and for their healing, has caused him to come under much criticism from colleagues. Yet his success in treating patients is remarkable.

When patients come to him he earnestly asks, "Do you *really* want to get well?" He repeats the same question several times during the office visit. If they consistently say they do, he tells them that many of their "idols" must go: sugar, salt, refined foods, caffeine, and junk foods to be sure. He recommends only small amounts of red meat and pork, because he feels they have too much fat and too many chemicals in them. He also suggests that his patients stay away from triple-decker burgers as they are too high in salt and carbohydrates, and because they represent a tendency for Americans to concentrate on excess protein intake.

Instead he recommends a diet consisting of 50 percent vegetables (half of those raw), 25 percent fruit, 15 percent grains and starches, and 10 percent protein (seeds, nuts, sprouts, eggs, milk, and meat). A diet is an individual thing, and we should consult a doctor in whom we have confidence, and who understands our needs. For example, I do not function well if I limit my protein intake to 10 percent of my total diet.

Stress-Producing Foods

"It is estimated that Americans eat more than 120 pounds of sugar every year" (Miller, *Prescription for,* p. 112). Our sweet tooths demand it! We get hooked on it early, as many baby formulas and baby foods are sweetened with sugar. Sugar acts as a preservative, so it's in everything from bouillon cubes to breads and canned vegetables. Nearly every store-bought, packaged product has some sugar in it.

Many packaged cereals—despite claims to be nutritious—are half sugar. We should be cautious of any product where sugar, corn syrup, corn sugar, or sucrose is among the first ingredients listed. Any one of those ingredients may be making you depressed, fatigued, irritable, restless, anxious, or obese. Sugar is even found in certain medicines, so check with your pharmacist to be safe.

All the sugar our bodies need for energy can be obtained from nutritious foods such as fruit. Even honey is not the best substitute for sugar. It causes the same rise in the blood sugar level as regular sugar.

"But if you feel you need to use a sweetener, use either raw honey or blackstrap molasses. Even an artificial sweetener is better than refined sugar. Make sure the honey you buy has not been strained or pasteurized. Remember, though ... even the Bible says 'it is not good to eat much honey'" (Prov. 25:27) (Miller *Prescription for,* p. 113).

Too much sugar in your diet can lead to hypoglycemia (low blood sugar) or diabetes (high blood sugar). In either case, the pancreas is not handling sugar properly. Symptoms range fron intense fatigue to an inability to concentrate. Diabetes can bring on blindness and kills over 300 thousand Americans every year.

When my stress symptoms were at their worst, I was advised to take the five-hour glucose-tolerance test. The blood sugar level is monitored by drinking a bottle of sugar water, and then drawing blood every hour for five hours. Some doctors are calling the glucose-tolerance test the most important one we will ever take. Generally, an imbalance in blood sugar can be corrected by eating properly.

My test revealed a borderline diabetic situation: very high blood sugar that could lead to diabetes if I didn't cut down on my intake of sugars and starches. (Most carbohydrates are turned into sugar in our bodies.)

I analyzed my diet. I usually did not eat breakfast, but if I did, it was donuts or toast with jam or jelly. The body simply must start the day with an intake of the right nutrients. The sugar and starches I consumed early in the morning may have given me a spurt out the door, but that energy output quickly fell off and soon brought on a stress attack. What I needed was some kind of protein in the morning. Cheese or peanut butter is good.

My lunches were mainly sugars and starches in the form of bread, chips, and cookies. Later in the day I had generous portions of tea, colas, potatoes, desserts, and more non-nutritious bread. Was it any wonder my body was not working up to capacity? Today I am convinced that of all the imbalances in my life, my diet was the most out of whack.

Another high stress-producer is caffeine, which is in coffee, tea, colas, chocolate, and even aspirin. It may give a brief energy spurt as sugar does, but in the end, it will create frazzled nerves and insomnia.

Refined manners are great, but refined and processed foods are deadly. Though packaged temptingly, these foods really harm our bodies. It has taken years for this to sink in. Today's mothers are becoming wise and are realizing that sugar, starches, and additives will only make Johnny fat, nervous, depressed, angry, moody, sick, and stress-ridden. On top of that, he'll have a mouth full of cavities.

Nutritional Disaster

When processed and refined products entered our society, they were heralded as "great innovations" and time-savers. In reality, they ushered in nutritional disaster. They have added to the stress-dilemma that is consuming the world today.

"The millers started to make these refined products for two reasons. They discovered they could sell the by-products of the refining process. For example, when wheat was stone-ground, there was no removal of the germ or the bran. It was sold as one product and had all the nutrients available to sustain life. The Bible refers to it as the staff of life, and it truly was.

"When they started to remove the germ, they discovered they could sell these items separately. The wheat germ could be sold to drug manufacturers. The bran could be sold to livestock producers. In other words, they could now sell several products: flour, wheat germ, and bran instead of just stone-ground wheat.

"The second reason is that it would last longer on the shelf. Economically, these reasons were very sound. Nutritionally, they were a disaster.

"So when you see that flour is 'enriched' or 'fortified,' don't believe it! . . . Things are so demineralized . . . [they] will not support life properly . . . not even insect life. They won't eat it . . . but we do!" (Miller, *Prescription for,* p. 110)

It takes nerve to call a product enriched or fortified after most of the important elements have been taken out. A few nutrients may be put into the product, but they are chemically synthesized nutrients. Be cautious of packaged breads, cereals, and snack foods like chips and crackers.

"So what should we eat?"

Here's a good rule to follow in nutrition: "If God made it, and man hasn't tampered with it, it's OK for you to eat. Think of all the things you can include: nuts, figs, dates, raisins, plums, apples, bananas, oranges, grapefruit, melons, and any other fruit in season. There are all sorts of vegetables: green peppers, lettuce, celery, radishes, spinach, squash, peas, potatoes, beans, zucchini, turnips, carrots, cabbage, mushrooms, and tomatoes" (Miller, *Prescription for,* p. 116).

Try to eat food that is as close to its natural state as possible, and that hasn't been processed by man. Eat uncooked fruits and vegetables frequently When foods are cooked, canned, or frozen, they lose many of their vitamins and minerals. But be sure to chew raw and coarse food well. This aids digestion and is of benefit to the intestinal tract. It also slows down mealtime and helps ease stress that way. Stressful people invariably eat too quickly. The digestive process starts with chewing and salivating. Eating on the run is the worst thing you can do if you have a sensitive stomach.

Other beneficial foods include cheese, eggs, poultry, fish, nuts, seeds, and whole-grain breads (without preservatives). If you *insist* on something sweet, use a little honey.

Vitamins and Stress

I cannot endorse vitamins enough. Before I began a program of vitamin therapy three years ago, six or eight times a year I was hit with a head cold which sent me to bed for three days and the symptoms lingered three weeks later.

Dr. Briggs points out that stress depletes our bodies of important vitamins and minerals, particularly water-soluble ones, and these are the vitamins we need when we're under stress. Caffeine, sugar, alcohol, and overrefined foods rob us of even more vitamins and minerals, and particularly those we need to deal with stress, depression, and anxiety.

Stress experts agree that to cope with the "anxious '80s" we need plenty of B12, B complex, B1 (thiamine), B6 (pyridoxine), C, potassium, zinc, calcium, magnesium, pantothenic acid, and E. The calcium magnesium combination has been called "nature's tranquilizer."

"Take vitamins in their natural form—not synthetic vitamins. . . . A synthetic substitute will never replace the natural one where vitamins are concerned. There is always something missing when man tries to improve on nature" (Miller, *Prescription for,* p. 124).

It is unfortunate that the health food and vitamin businesses have received bad press. Self-proclaimed experts have come on the scene in the last decade. Many of them lack the proper physiological training and their accurate warnings against food additives, preservatives, and sugar have been mixed with half-truths in the area of nutrition. Some health food stores offer books on TM, yoga, Eckankar, self-hypnosis, and occult adventures. Buyers not wanting to overlook any area that might improve health naively get caught in this, but beware. Sugar robs you of vitamins, but yoga and TM may lead to something that could steal your soul.

Also be cautious of the term "holistic health." If it is used in the Christian sense, fine. Today, however, it can be associated with Eastern religions, Christian Science, and the occult.

Once you've established yourself nutritionally (and you might want to talk with a professional in the field), here are more tips to help you make positive changes in your eating habits:

• Avoid other activities when you eat. Don't read or watch television.

• Don't think you are doing yourself a favor by not eating all day and then having a feast at dinnertime. It's been said we should "eat like a king at breakfast time, like a queen at lunchtime, and like a pauper at dinnertime."

• If you must bring problem foods into the house, keep them out of sight and out of reach.

• Never do your grocery shopping on an empty stomach.

• Plan your meals ahead of time.

• Have a grocery list and buy only what's on your list.

• Try to take just enough money so you won't buy unnecessary, tempting items.

• Try serving your meals on smaller dishes, and it will look like there is more food than there actually is. Serve yourself last, but don't think you have to clean up the platter!

• Eat slowly so that you don't finish first. You may be tempted to take second helpings to be eating with everyone else.

• Keep a good supply of carrots, celery, cauliflower, fruit, and other safe snacks in the refrigerator.

• If you tend to eat because of loneliness, depression, or boredom, keep a handy list of friends to call rather than laying into the potato chips.

• Help those following a nutritional eating plan by giving encouragement and praise.

Avoid foods that offer you nothing but trouble. God demanded high caliber animal sacrifices from the Israelites. As living sacrifices for Him, we should be in good condition, and that's impossible apart from a balanced diet. If you can't do it yourself, have a professional map out the right nutritional program for your body and lifestyle.

Slow Down, World!

Slow down, world!
Halt your maddening pace
   to and fro,
Going nowhere;
On the move,
   yet directionless.
Running frantic;
Pursuing elusive goals
   and leaving in the dust
   a needy soul
   who wanted just 10 minutes
      of your time
   to listen.
Can't you hear the deafening roar
   of humanity
   in need of just one person
   who will forsake the pursuit
      of fun and games,
   and say
   by listening,
      "I love you"?

11
Personalities
Come in Two Types

Some personality characteristics contribute to a poorly balanced lifestyle. Drs. Meyer Friedman and Ray Rosenman discovered this while dealing with patients suffering from heart disease. In their book *Type A Behavior and Your Heart,* they categorize people in A and B types. Type A people sit on the edge of the chairs in the doctor's office, wanting to return to work as soon as possible. Type B people are more relaxed and generally slower paced. They listen to what the doctor prescribes and live accordingly. Type A people must work to avoid stressful habits, while Type B people are prone to shun stress. Here are more traits of both types.

Which Are You?
"You are a Type A personality if you:
- Explosively accentuate key words in your ordinary speech.
- Always move, walk, and eat rapidly. You measure success by how fast things are done.
- Feel impatient with the rate at which most events take place.
- Indulge in multiple thought or performance: doing more than one thing at a time or thinking about your next day's appointments while someone is talking to you.
- Find it difficult to refrain from talking, are preoccupied with

talking about self, or drop out of a conversation to think about yourself.
- Usually feel guilty when you relax; have great difficulty doing nothing.
- Seldom see the sunset, flowers, or trees.
- Attempt to schedule more and more in less and less time.
- Resort to such nervous gestures as kicking the foot, clenching the jaw, or banging the hand on a table.
- Rush your speech.
- Hate to wait in line or be delayed in traffic.
- Read mostly summaries.
- Like leading, but not following.
- Take over the work of others because you feel you can do it better or faster.

"You are a Type B personality if you:
- Have none of the Type A traits.
- Never suffer from a sense of urgency with its accompanying impatience.
- Have little need to discuss your accomplishments.
- Play for fun and relaxation rather than to be competitive and exhibit superiority.
- Can relax without guilt and work without agitation" (Fawcett Crest Books, pp. 100-103).

If you are Type A and your family has a history of hypertension and other stress-related diseases, Jane and I encourage you to work at adopting the Type B personality. It is possible to change! It may take months, even years, to make the switch, but it *can* be done, and for some the change may be a matter of life and death. I have a long way to go, but through prayer and practice I'm learning to relax and see life at five miles an hour.

Want to Change?

You too can alter your Type A personality by:
- Living with unfinished tasks.
- Scheduling a reasonable number of appointments or tasks in a day.

- Learning to say no to projects that will overload you.
- Slowing down your walk, speech, and eating.
- Finding time every day to relax.
- Leaving details to someone else.
- Forcing yourself to wait without being annoyed.
- Delegating responsibility to others and accepting their work.

You will feel better and people will feel better about you.

12
The Tyranny
of Time

A sinister philosophy pervading the world today says that "time is money."

Christians have pet slogans too. One says, "Every minute must count for the Lord." Many Christians hardly know what free time is. While Christians should not work every minute, we need to recognize that our time differs from that of non-Christians. Tim Hansel puts it this way:

"For the Christian there is no such thing as free time. All of the Christian's time is redeemed and belongs to the One who has set us free" (*When I Relax, I Feel Guilty,* David C. Cook, p. 68).

Like other resources, time is allotted to us by God, and He does call us to be good stewards of it. But God knows exactly how much time we have; if we are in His will, there will be enough time to do all that He wants us to do. He does not want time to be a tyrant!

The psalmist says, "Teach us to number our days, that we may apply our hearts unto wisdom" (Ps. 90:12, KJV). He advocates the wise use of time.

"People feel guilty about time and how they use it. It is peculiar that the Christian, who has been set free to discover the wonder of God in all the universe, should deny himself or herself that glorious experience by feeling guilty in taking the time to do so" (James

Johnson, *How to Enjoy Life and Not Feel Guilty,* Harvest House, p. 103).

Even the church gets caught up in the tyranny of time. Some churches have activities nearly every night of the week. Sundays are crammed with several worship and teaching times, committee meetings, and entertaining. There is little holy quietness on the "day of rest."

Hurry, Hurry

In his book *Zorba the Greek,* Nikos Kazantzakes poignantly comments on the hurry sickness of the 20th century: "I remember one morning when I discovered a cocoon in the bark of a tree, just as the butterfly was making a hole in its case and preparing to come out. I waited awhile, but it was too long appearing and I was impatient. I bent over it and breathed on it to warm it. I warmed it as quickly as I could and the miracle began to happen before my eyes faster than life. The case opened. The butterfly started slowly crawling out and I shall never forget my horror when I saw how its wings were folded back and crumpled; the wretched butterfly tried with its whole trembling body to unfold them.

"Bending over it I tried to help it with my breath, in vain. It needed to be hatched out patiently. And the unfolding of the wings should be a gradual process in the sun. Now it was too late. My breath had forced the butterfly to appear all crumpled before its time. It struggled desperately and a few seconds later, it died in the palm of my hand.

"That little body is, I do believe, the greatest weight I have on my conscience. For I realize today that it is a mortal sin to violate the great laws of nature. We should not hurry. We should not be impatient. But we should confidently obey the eternal rhythm.

"If only that butterfly could always flutter before me to show me the way" (Simon and Schuster, p. 59).

Mismanaging Your Time?

Some experts believe we waste as much as 80 percent of our time. Christians may not waste their time as much as they mismanage it.

Try these ideas from the time management seminars that Jane and I conduct.

- At the start of each day, make a list of the projects that need to be accomplished. Group the projects by priority: "A" most important, "C" least important. Tackle the prime projects during the time of day when you are at your peak. If "C" doesn't get finished, relax! We do need to know God's priorities and to determine what is necessary in our day.
- Paul's method of coping with time was to be single-minded (Rom. 8; Gal. 5) (see chapter 13).
- Become God-pleasers rather than man-pleasers (see chapter 13). Learn to say no to some assignments. Don't overextend yourself. Be realistic with your time. Recognize too that God can enable you to do more work in shorter time, can arrange circumstances so that some activities are slowed down while others are speeded up.
- Be careful not to do the work of other people (see chapter 13). It may deprive them of doing what God wants them to do.
- Let others know when you need help; they may not be aware of it. And when you do share the load, dismiss thoughts that this job won't get done right. Let God be the perfectionist, not you.
- Divide big and overwhelming projects into smaller ones. I learned this principle early in my book-writing career. I can not easily focus all my attention on the 200 typewritten pages needed for a book. Instead I approach a book in sections, and I feel that I've reached a milestone when I finish one of these sections.
- Check your day for "time-wasters." Do you talk on the telephone without setting a time limit?
- Do you watch TV or read the paper much longer than is necessary? See if a half-hour news broadcast and one weekly news magazine doesn't inform you sufficiently.
- Do you let the kids' interruptions run your day?
- Is your schedule so disorganized that it causes you to waste time?

Don't procrastinate. With each delay it becomes harder to get started!

- Allow more time than you think you need for activities and appointments. If you schedule too tightly, you'll be burned out in no time. You will always be in a hurry. Get up a little earlier to give yourself more time. Unless your job absolutely demands it, stop telling yourself that everything has to be done by 5 P.M. The 5 P.M. frenzy takes its toll.
- Occasionally go to places where you know you will have to wait. Then learn to wait without fidgeting and looking at your watch.
- Read things that demand patience and your entire attention.
- See if your lifestyle can be made less complicated. If your hair requires too much attention every morning, get another hair style.
- About three times a day remind yourself that life is always unfinished. You are finished only when your life ends.

Set Goals

When counseling time-ravaged Christians we have advised that every six months it is good to establish long-term goals in regard to our families, our jobs/ministries, and our personal lives. Under each category, write down no more than three goals for that six-month period. At the beginning of each week, take a piece of paper and write out the same categories, setting three *smaller* goals for that time period (but keeping the long-term goals in mind).

To narrow the process even further, write *today's goals* on another paper and ask the Lord's help in completing them for the day. (But keep your expectation realistic.) If at the end of the day you do not complete the goals, put them at the top of the next day's list. Frequently check your daily goals and your weekly goals to see if in trying to meet them, you're using your time wisely.

But be flexible. There should be some *kairos* ("spontaneous, opportune times") that you'll never forget. There also will be such daily interruptions of life as unexpected phone calls and visitors. God does not want us to "toil and spin" so rigidly that we have no joy or freedom in surprises. We must allow the Lord to work through us, enabling us to be more productive and fruitful.

Perhaps we cannot actually *manage* time, but we can *use* what we have more efficiently. We all have the same 24 hours, 1,440 minutes or 86,400 seconds. The difference comes in how each of us deals with that time. God has given us time to accomplish what He wants us to do! If we have far more to do than we have time for, we may have chosen to undertake some things God never intended we do.

Time is a precious commodity and should be handled with care. For Christians, however, I believe there can be a kind of "sovereign efficiency" of time if we stay in tune to God, and have enough flexibility in our schedules for God to "arrange" the circumstances of that day in order that the time is used to best advantage.

I have found too that when we are generous (though balanced) with our time (and money), God specializes in giving it back to us in an even greater proportion.

Countdown

No time.

Forgive us, Lord,
For making life a marathon race.
For chomping at the bit at the starting gate
Listening for the sound of the gun,
Only to chase around in circles.

No time . . .
To be about my Father's business,
But time enough to shoot 18 holes
Or spend a weekend in the woods.

No time . . .
To really listen to a friend;
Just time enough to nod and pretend
I've assimilated his plea to be understood.
But I never heard,
Not even one word.

Forgive this frantic pace, Lord.
May these gifts not be taken away
Before we learn to take time,
Or before,
In the end,
Time is no more.

Amen.

13
Ways to
Cope with Stress

In addition to maintaining a balance of rest, relaxation, leisure, exercise, and proper nutrition, there are hundreds of techniques for dealing with stress. Some are too expensive for most people; other methods are not practical. Such methods as the use of alcohol, tranquilizers, and food to soothe the nerves and emotions are as harmful to the body as the stress is. We've become a society that heads for the refrigerator and the medicine chest when we feel stress. A quick "sizing up" of Christians frequently indicates that we handle our stress with food. Other people slip into a fantasy world and are absorbed by the TV. The average American watches five hours of television a day, and much of that is for escape purposes.

A new coping device is Video Wallpaper. It's a product that turns the TV set into an electronic sedative. It consists of 14 half-hour video cassettes containing mother nature's most tranquilizing sights and sounds. Among them are "Flowing Falls"—a lush cove fed by a majestic waterfall; "Clouds of Peace"—slow-moving clouds against a deep-blue sky; and "Reflections"—a pond shimmering in the afternoon sun, complete with songbirds. Video Wallpaper can be played on any standard video cassette machine. Some hospitals are piping it over closed circuit TV systems to alleviate patient anxiety and to help treat stress-related psychological disorders.

Practical Suggestions

I'd like to deal with some practical ways of coping with stress and to look at men and women of the Bible who did or did not cope with the stress of their day.

• First, you need to recognize and define what causes stress in your life. Keep track of your stress quotient; everyone's is different. If your body says you are pushing beyond its limits, pull back. Accept some limits in your life. Pace yourself and learn to say no. Don't try to be the "bionic woman" or "superman." Once you establish your stress quotient, take risks so that you will be challenged, but not so many that you are overwhelmed.

• Avoid clustering major life changes. (See chart on page 90.) If you can see that your week holds too many high-stress projects, rearrange your schedule, if possible.

• Focus on pleasing God more than man. Adam wanted to please Eve rather than stand firm in what he knew was truth. Eve, under stress, listened to the serpent and sinned. Mankind has paid for Adam's and Eve's inability to handle stress.

• Learn to live with imperfection in yourself and in other people, projects, and churches. Those who strive to be perfect, according to all the stress experts, are the most likely candidates for burnout.

• Maintain a strong support group of friends and family members. Among them find a few (even one or two) with whom you can be open. Use one another as "safety valves" by sharing, confiding, and encouraging one another. Be as concerned about their stress and trials as you are your own. (See chapter 16.)

Joshua and Caleb handled their stress by being *encouragers*. They saw the same obstacles that the other spies saw, but they came back saying, "We *can* take the land."

My pastor responds to "How are you?" by answering, "Always good!" No matter what the circumstances, he is "always good" and thereby encourages those around him who may be yielding to the stress of the day.

• Develop an attitude of gratitude rather than self-pity. Thank God for all things and assume they're in your life for your ultimate good. (Also see chapter 14.)

Job did this. In spite of his traumas, he praised God. He didn't blame his circumstances on God. He clearly didn't enjoy his predicament, but he accepted it, though he asked why. Jacob, in contrast, gave in to self-pity when he was told that his favorite son, Joseph, had been killed. He wept far beyond the normal period of mourning. When some sought to comfort him, he said, "I will go down into the grave unto my son" (Gen. 37:35). Stress surely took its toll on Jacob.

Paul was frequently deprived of food, water, clothing, and other comforts. He was attacked by the Jews and the Gentiles, grieved by the squabbles between the brethren, and frequently beaten and imprisoned. But instead of going on a self-pity trip, he focused on the fact that no amount of stress and discomfort could separate him from the love of Christ. He testified: "In all things we overwhelmingly conquer through Him who loved us . . . neither death . . . nor principalities . . . nor height nor depth, nor any other created thing [can] separate us from the love of God (Rom. 8:37-39).

The Apostle Paul learned to be content in all circumstances (Phil. 4:11). It didn't happen overnight. He learned to think on what was true, lovely, and good, and to "rejoice" even when he was under stress. He concentrated on God's goodness to him rather than on his circumstances.

• Learn to have a good self-image and accept what you can't change. You will fail now and then. The world may not always give you a standing ovation, you won't always be understood, your motives may be questioned.

• Be expressive. Laughter and tears are excellent stress relievers. Jeremiah handled his stress by weeping and crying out to God. In the Garden of Gethsemane, Jesus knew His time was at hand and He wept and prayed. Laughter is a good outlet: "A merry heart doeth good like a medicine" (Prov. 17:22, KJV). Learn to see humor in the pieces of life that don't fit together.

And if you can't express yourself orally, try keeping a journal or a diary. Pour out your feelings in it. When anger, frustration, or disappointment are bottled up, they're going to pop out through ulcers and heart disease.

• Control your input. Far too much time is given over to the bad news of our day. Through television and other media, we are bombarded with scandals, riots, disasters, violence, crime, and human misery. Limit the amount that you absorb without sticking your head in the sand.

• Learn to delegate and share responsibility. Moses did not have enough hours in the day to deal with all the problems the people created. His father-in-law, Jethro, put his finger on the real issue: Moses was not sharing the responsibilities. He took too much on himself. Jethro scolded him, "You will surely wear out... for the task is too heavy for you; you cannot do it alone" (Ex. 18:13-27).

Lean on the Lord. Trust Him with all your heart. The Psalmist David conquered not only Goliath but also stress. He had to cope with attacks on his life by King Saul, a lion, a bear, and a host of other unnamed assailants. But David knew how to put his trust in the Lord and avoid high blood pressure: "The Lord is my light and my salvation: whom shall I fear? The Lord is the defense of my life; whom shall I dread? When evildoers came upon me to devour my flesh, my adversaries and my enemies, they stumbled and fell. Though a host encamp against me, my heart will not fear; though war arise against me, in spite of this I shall be confident" (Ps. 27:1-3).

"When I am afraid, I will put my trust in Thee. In God, whose Word I praise, in God I have put my trust; I shall not be afraid. What can mere man do to me?" (Ps. 56:3-4)

Esther, in her plight to save her people, handled her stress by fasting and earnestly seeking the Lord. She exercised her faith, knowing that she might have to die, yet trusting God to deliver her and her people.

Shadrach, Meshach, and Abednego were thrown into a furnace, yet they were so confident God would save them they ultimately emerged without even the smell of smoke on their clothing.

In like manner Daniel "believed in his God" (Dan. 6:23, KJV). He knew God would deliver him from the lions' den. Our lions' den may be ill health, financial peril, or family difficulties, but the principle of faith still exists.

Abraham had two choices when it came to sacrificing his beloved son. He could wallow in self-pity and refuse to obey God, or he could exercise his faith and rest in the difficult assignment. Because Abraham obeyed, God established the Abrahamic covenant. Who knows how many blessings we miss when we don't allow God to test us and try our faith!

Nobody witnessed the power of Jesus like the disciples. But even their faith was shaky. While Jesus slept in their boat, a storm began to rage. The disciples panicked, certain they were going to perish, and took the situation into their own hands. Jesus rebuked them and calmed the sea.

We often panic and become stressful because we are certain we can't handle whatever is about to come on us. We forget to lean on God, to rest in Him, and know that He will not give us more than we can handle.

• Cut down on excessive noise. Our generation is bombarded with freeway noise, air raid sirens, jet aircraft, honking, screeching traffic, police sirens, and the like. Much we can't control, but in some cases we can do something.

Some years ago I realized I had made a dreadful mistake by renting an apartment near the Minneapolis/St. Paul airport. Jets streaked over my head night and day, and I seldom got more than five or six hours of sleep. Everyone told me that in a few weeks I would be used to the noise, even though my walls literally vibrated every time a jet went overhead.

After a month of that kind of torture, I went to the trouble of moving again. I knew my limitations were being stretched too far; I had exceeded my stress quotient! For me, the only healthy thing to do was to change environment.

The sound of music can either heal us or make us ill. Someone once said that you "can't sing and worry at the same time." David knew that whenever Saul became distressed, music would relax his spirits. But I am sure it was soothing music and not that of some of the contemporary rock groups.

Scientific tests have indicated that intense rhythms and beats are body manipulators, and that people can be either soothed by the sounds or destroyed and maddened. Little wonder that many homes are tension-ridden: the stereo is blaring for several hours a day. The atmosphere is electric with stress, when a simple flick of the switch could reduce it all. Choose music carefully: avoid words that create deep emotions and that build to a crescendo.

• Give up the obsession today's society has with numbers: the quantity of things done, quotas met, sales made. Avoid unnecessary competition and focus instead on the *quality* of life.

• Be single-minded. Paul accomplished more in his lifetime than most of us would in two lifetimes and he revealed his secret in "This one thing I do" (Phil. 3:13, KJV).

Jesus may have had this in mind when he told Martha, "You are worried and bothered about so many things: but only a few things are necessary, really only one" (Luke 10:41, KJV).

• Don't move on to a second project till you've finished the first. This also applies to leisure-time activities. Don't start reading a new book if you're only half finished with two others. I've learned now not to accept a book from a friend if I know I can't get at it for weeks or months. When my book table gets piled high, I come under too much stress.

• Be willing to compromise. To insist you are right, to never give in, only creates tension.

• Always do what is right, ethical, and legal. We feel great stress whenever we must "cover up."

• Practice moving more slowly! Slow your speech, your walk, and your eating.

• Employ "safety-valves" at your place of work as well. Take a walk on your lunch break or do a few exercises. Find a quiet place to talk to the Lord. Say nice things to your fellow employees. Don't let your job control you. Such stress-relieving activities at work will not cut into your productive working time. In fact they will increase your efficiency and at 5 P.M. you will still have energy left.

Space does not allow me to expand on all of the biblical examples. Ask God to personalize a Bible character for you, that you might learn from him or her. When I did that, God impressed Elijah on me.

Elijah vividly demonstrates the importance of taking care of ourselves (1 Kings 19). Often God's answer to the treatment of our stress is so simple. Elijah was frightfully tired and depressed: a classic case of burnout, when God provided food, rest, and a change of scenery. When Elijah was overworked and despairing, Satan had moved in to take advantage of him, but when he was rested and fed, God gave him a new assignment. The spirit of expectancy related to his new assignment lifted Elijah's depression. Note that God did not give him the assignment till Elijah's bodily needs were met.

Measure Your Stress

Stress experts have come up with the Stress Index Chart. "Life change unit points" were assigned to typical life events. See for yourself where you stand. Add the points to get your score. If you score less than 150, you're doing well; between 150 and 300 you probably have too much stress in your life because of life changes; over 300 you're headed for a major health change.

The Stress of Adjusting to Change

Rank	Event	Stress Points
1	Death of spouse	100
2	Divorce	73
3	Marital separation	65
4	Jail term	63
5	Death of a close family member	63
6	Personal injury or illness	53
7	Marriage	50
8	Fired from job	47
9	Marital reconciliation	45
10	Retirement	45
11	Change in health of family member	44
12	Pregnancy	40
13	Sex difficulties	39
14	Gain of new family member	39
15	Business readjustment	39
16	Change in financial state	38
17	Death of a close friend	37

18	Change of work	36
19	Change in number of marital arguments	35
20	Mortgage over $10 thousand	31
21	Foreclosure of mortgage or loan	30
22	Change in responsibility at work	29
23	Son or daughter leaving home	29
24	Trouble with in-laws	29
25	Outstanding personal achievement	28
26	Wife begins or stops work	26
27	Beginning or end of school	26
28	Change in living conditions	25
29	Revision of personal habits	24
30	Trouble with boss	23
31	Change in work hours or conditions	20
32	Change in residence	20
33	Change in schools	20
34	Change in recreation	19
35	Change in church activities	19
36	Change in social activities	18
37	Mortgage or loan less than $10,000	17
38	Change in sleeping habits	16
39	Change in number of family get-togethers	15
40	Change in eating habits	15
41	Vacation	13
42	Christmas	12
43	Minor violations of the law	11

Masquerade

I'm hiding, Lord,
  and I'm tired of the masquerade.
The costume bag has been exhausted.
The masks are worn and ragged.
365 days of Halloween is not a treat.

I'm hiding because I'm frightened . . .
  of the smiles covering tears
  and paint covering years,
  and just the whole game
  of hide and seek.

This morning, Lord,
  I put the costume bag in the attic.
This afternoon I must venture out
  with no cover-ups,
  tricks,
  or gimmicks.
Just the timid, sensitive, caring individual
  You made me,
  seeking perhaps just one more
  who wants out of the game.
Together we could go through life unafraid,
  seeing not only the surface,
  but beneath;
Sharing even the daydreams,
  and the crazy, childlike fantasies
  of life together.

Lord, smooth out the rough edges
  of the real me.
I've never played that role before.

Amen.

14
Praise
Reduces Stress

Martin Luther often stated, "I'm going to work, work, work today from morning to night. I'm going to work *so* much, I'm going to spend the first three hours of the day in prayer."

Time alone with God will fortify and renew us. It is imperative in order to survive in our generation.

God charged Joshua with the importance of meditating. "This book of the law shall not depart from your mouth, but you shall meditate on it day and night so that you may be careful to do according to all that is written in it; for then you will make your way prosperous, and then you will have success" (Josh. 1:8).

According to this passage, the casual Christian will have a difficult road because he will not be familiar with God's ways and His Book, and he will probably be bound up in the stress of the world. On the other hand, those who are willing to meditate on God, *listen* earnestly to His "still, small voice," seek His face, and most important, praise and worship Him, will find deliverance from the destructive forces of stress!

I emphasized listening because it has become a lost art. Somehow it got swallowed up in the vacuum cleaner of technology. Oh we may listen to the television, or to a baseball game, but we don't genuinely *hear* God or others very well. (See chapter 16.) In many conversations we're often wishing folks would finish their sentences so that we can jump in with our ideas. We even finish people's sentences so we can talk sooner. We're hurt when people don't really listen to us, but it doesn't hurt our consciences when we tune them out or when we do all the talking.

And so it is with the Lord. We complain, get angry, and frequently give Him a piece of our mind. We seldom are still, waiting for His direction, wisdom, or comfort.

"We must be introduced to the delicate and vanishing art of listening. This demands of us a willingness to sit quietly at the feet of God, in His personal, dynamic presence. We must be willing to shut out all the noises and distractions of the scene about us, and in the stillness of a living faith, await the touch of God" (John Powell, *A Reason to Live! A Reason to Die!* Argus Communications, p. 148).

Try Praise During Stress

The principle is this: Quality time alone with God will set us apart from the world and the stresses of life.

Some people have the misconception that a "quiet time" should be only a passive, meditative attitude, but that leaves out a key ingredient—*praise*. The psalmist wrote, "His praise shall continually be in my mouth" (Ps. 34:1). When we praise God, our stress and anxiety ease.

A good illustration of this is the story of Jehoshaphat (2 Chron. 20). Several countries were sending armies to fight him. When he heard the news he was frightened and he "set himself to seek the Lord" (2 Chron. 20:3, KJV). He gathered the people together and they all prayed. Jehoshaphat stated the problem: he was downright scared because they were so outnumbered. He acknowledged he didn't know what to do, but he said, "Our eyes are upon Thee" (v. 12).

After they prayed, God spoke through a man named Jahaziel: "Hearken ye, all Judah . . . and thou King Jehoshaphat. Thus saith the Lord unto you: 'Be not afraid nor dismayed by reason of this great multitude; for the battle is not yours but God's'" (v. 15).

We need to remember this principle for the situations that produce stress, tension, fear, and anxiety in the decade of the '80s. We need to pray, "Lord, these battles are not mine; they're Yours. I acknowledge this and I praise You for Your power to deal with them."

The next thing that happened to Jehoshaphat and his men is most interesting. Several groups stood up to praise the God of Israel. They knew they were going to face the stress of battle, and they needed a shield of praise. So Jehoshaphat appointed singers to praise the Lord as they marched out to meet the enemy. And when they began to sing, the Lord set ambushments against the men who had come against Judah. When Jehoshaphat's men praised the Lord, He moved to deal with the causes of their stress.

Maintaining an Attitude of Praise

Too often we say, "Lord, take away this stressful situation: the problem with my boss; my wayward teenager; my annoying physical malady. Then I will sing and praise You!"

Thanking God in advance and maintaining a continual attitude of praise does not come easy. You might as well acknowledge to God that it is hard to do, but by faith you're going to do it because it pleases Him.

When David fled from his enemies (1 Sam. 21—22), he found safety in a cave. Scripture says 400 other men joined him there, and all of them were distressed and discontent. Can you picture David saying to them, "I will bless the Lord at all times; His praise shall continually be in my mouth. My soul shall make its boast in the Lord . . . O magnify the Lord with me and let us exalt His name together" (Ps. 34:1-3). All 400 men could have turned on him, for they wanted to enjoy self-pity, or at the very least, complain about their circumstances and the many injustices in life. David had learned that praise was the best way to handle stress and fear. It didn't come naturally, but he had lots of practice. Read the Psalms.

I am convinced that time alone with God is the most important part of the day. We simply cannot deal adequately with our own stress, nor can we reach out to love, forgive, and heal others if we aren't tuned-in to the One who makes us capable of doing that.

Set aside a specific time every day to meditate, worship, listen, and praise. Experiment with the time. First thing in the morning might not work out, so try it at midday or late at night (though your day will be fortified if you begin it with God). I have a friend who locks herself in the bathroom and reads her Bible in the bathtub. It is the only way she can get away from the commotion of her home and five children. That might not work for you, but it was a made-to-order innovation for her.

Don't set a limit on time alone with the Lord. Allow enough time for the Spirit of God to speak to you. If your quiet time is rigid, and you insist on reading only one chapter a day, and praying only three minutes, you're not allowing freedom for the Holy Spirit to speak to your heart and fortify you for the day's stress. I have often found that I am more free to concentrate on God if I exercise or practice some relaxation exercises before my quiet time. This helps clear my mind and relax my body; I feel more alert. When stress is reduced by exercise or relaxation, my mind and heart are more quiet.

Write Down Your Blessings

Keep a prayer journal so you can see how God answers your prayers, and the prayers of others. This will encourage you and motivate you to make this time an important part of your day. You'll find yourself writing down blessings that you never even prayed for, but God in His goodness blessed you with them anyway.

Every day list the things for which you are thankful. And enthusiastically praise Him for each. Consider including a song in your time alone with God. Scripture songs are popular now. They're worshipful and they praise the Lord. We can praise Him with our voices, and with instruments.

So make it a daily priority to come humbly before God; focus and meditate on Him; express your love to Him, as well as your praise and worship. Bless the Lord!

Once you learn to do this faithfully, you will see more changes in your life. The stresses may still confront you, but your reaction to them will be different. The stress will no longer control you. Allow the Spirit of God to renew you daily and He will enable you to control daily stress, strain, fear, and anxiety.

Candid Camera

Great God, You know me through and through!
I've tried to cover up.
I've tried to camouflage
I've played games with myself
    and with You.
I've fooled a lot of people.
For a day I even fooled myself.

But Lord, You've seen the real me,
    and yet You go on
        loving
        forgiving
        and picking up the pieces.

There's no place I can escape.
There's no place to hide.
There's no thought that eludes You.
You know my heart before it feels.
You know my words before they are sentences.
You know my motives
    and prejudices
    and selfish goals.
You know the hurt behind the smile;
    the jealousy behind the handshake;
    and the bitterness behind the pat on the back.

It's all there in vivid, living color.
The candid camera to my soul.

And the wonder of wonders,
    is that none of it sways Your love
    and Your care for me
    even one degree!

Amen.

15
Stress and
the Single Adult

Statistics reveal more single adults in this generation than ever before. The divorced, never marrieds, widows, and widowers, now make up one-third of our population.

We read in the Bible about single people. Jeremiah was commanded by God not to marry (Jer. 16). John the Baptist, Jesus, Paul, and Barnabas were single. Of the 12 Apostles, only Peter is said to have been married (Mark 1:30; 1 Cor. 9:5). Mary and Martha and Lazarus were single, as well as Mary Magdalene. Others, such as Naomi, encountered the death of a spouse and were left as single parents.

I've spent 15 adult years as a single, and I know how singles think. One hundred different lines run through their heads. Some feel they have been cheated; others that they are losers.

"I think I'm just the innocent victim of the lower birth rate," commented another. "Or a victim of the Viet Nam War. It took too many young men."

Friends fuel self-pity fires with such comments as, "You are just not complete without a mate" (though millions of people with mates still feel incomplete). Too often the church contributes to a single person's stress. Church is clearly a family affair with its family night, its young marrieds and "pair-ables" Sunday School classes. It reinforces the idea in the single's mind that he or she is a marginal member of a couple-oriented society. Many single adults leave a church service feeling more lonely and depressed than when they came in. The message they hear may be nonverbal, but they come away with the distinct impression that this is a couple's world.

On many occasions I have been afflicted with single stress syndrome. It hits me full force when I have to deal with car problems, when the roof leaks, or when I have to repair equipment. It does another number on me at income tax time or when I try to understand the fine print on an insurance policy. I'm agitated when my married friends are dropped off at the door while I park the car and wade through the rain puddles. I easily feel shortchanged when an affectionate couple sits in front of me in church. Because I've no one to help me with decisions, that process can devastate me. And it's worse to be sick alone or to face the prospect of growing old alone. Simply stated, *sharing* a burden greatly reduces everyday stress.

Loneliness Is Stressful

The loneliness factor in the life of the single is the biggest stress-producer. During World War II, it was discovered that the most effective type of punishment or torture was solitary confinement. More recent studies show that lonely people live shorter lives than others. While there is healing in human contact, loneliness can be downright unhealthy.

I know that the pain of loneliness is severe, for God created us to need one another. He may not have created everyone for marriage, but He did create everyone for love. We *all* need love. Tests are starting to show that the cause of much emotional illness is the inability to form close human relationships—even in marriage. Though in friendship the intimate relationship will be nonsexual, caring and warmth are needed.

We don't have to experience loneliness unless we choose not to make the effort to build close relationships. If we make such a choice, our fear of the responsibility of friendship is greater than our fear of loneliness.

Through friendship, intimacy is available in varying degrees to everyone. Jonathan and David had a close friendship. No doubt each was a "significant other"; each probably considered the other's good as much as his own. A "significant other" will miss us when we're away and long for our company.

Families Can Minister to Singles

I believe the church has some responsibility to singles. The church has been created as a body—as a family in which all are loved—and the families in this corporate family can minister love, healing, and acceptance to the single adult.

I shall be eternally grateful for a few families who have done this for me. In word and action they have let me know their home is mine and I am welcome at their dinner table during holiday times when singleness is particularly painful. I have shown up at their homes at 3 A.M. and been received with a smile. I have called them at late hours when my car has broken down. They have let me know in many ways that I am not alone, even though the enemy tries to impress me with my aloneness. I was never able to find this kind of relationship in the world, but I have enjoyed it with a few families in the church.

Perhaps the stress of my singleness cannot be compared to that of the divorcee, widow, and single parent. Once again, the church must come to the rescue. Grief is a major stress-producer, and grief probably causes a person to withdraw rather than to interact. The church needs to reach out to these people who may otherwise sit at home and feel sorry for themselves, indulging in resentment, despair, and depression. The stresses are immense. Gone is the love and affirmation they had received from a spouse. They have doubts and fears. Will they become a burden to their friends and children? Can they manage finances alone? Should they consider remarriage?

The divorced woman (or man) goes through the trauma of rejection, anger, guilt, fear, distrust, and sometimes shock. To be vulnerable again may be difficult. The church can be their "support group"—not a fancy program run by a psychologist in a hospital setting—but one made up of individuals and families who provide close friendships for the never-married and formerly-married. The "family for singles" concept in the church can become the best supportive community for the Christian. It adds the depth and closeness necessary for a balanced Christian lifestyle.

Families who never try interacting with singles are missing the new dimension a single can give by being an "aunt," "daughter," or "sister." We all can be happier, more balanced people with this kind of interaction.

My advice to singles is to communicate to families—let them know you want to be a part of their lives. Unless they read this book or other books with a similar message, they may not realize that singles desire the fellowship of families. Till I explained this to some married people, they assumed that I as a single adult would be uncomfortable in activities with couples. I tell married couples to treat us singles as people first and singles second. As I see it, loneliness produces isolation, stress, and sickness. Intimacy with the entire family of God produces wholeness, health, and a feeling of well-being.

If singleness is a prison, then I believe it is one that we have *chosen.* The single adult is bound only by chains of his own choosing.

Empathy

Oh, did I risk today, Lord!
I tiptoed into dangerous territory.
Admittedly I closed my eyes and had
    to be pushed,
    but in I went
    and I'm here to tell You it wasn't easy.

I reached out to love,
    but no one accepted it.
They turned away,
    themselves unable to risk.

I reached out to share what I had,
    and it was refused,
    as people glanced at me skeptically,
    unsure of my motives.

I reached out to bear a burden for another,
    and they turned away,
    saying they could not confide in me.

I reached out to give myself away,
    and I nearly had to pay someone
    to accept me!

I don't know if I can ever risk again, Father!
It was so painful.
I fear I could duck back under
    that proverbial turtle shell
    and just let the world go by me,
    giving no thought or care to it
That is, unless You empower me
    to reach out and risk again,
    and again, and yet another time.

Come to think of it,
    very few wanted what You had to offer either.
I guess You know how I feel. Amen.

Thanks for Special Friends, Lord!

I'm childishly exuberant today, Lord,
    and all that happened was
    that I received a valentine!

But it was special . . . from a special friend,
    and it said that
    I was loved
    and understood
    and that I was missed.

You've given me a good friend, Lord . . .
One who hears what I am not saying;
One who reads between the lines
    and hears the unspoken requests of my heart;
One who soothes the nagging pain of
    not being understood.
A friend whose joy is contagious,
    whose laugh is communicable.
Who says at all times,
    "I know how you feel."

My friend loves me in spite of emotional
    reactions in life,
    similar to a roller coaster!

Thanks for special friends, Lord.
There's a lot of You in them . . .
    Your love
    Your patience
    Your understanding.

Today I know that I matter
    To You and to my friend!

It is a good feeling to be loved. Amen.

16
Stress
and Friends

The theme of intimacy is carried over into this chapter. Millions of people never have had a close friend with whom they could share their deepest feelings. People are forced to see a psychiatrist or counselor because they don't have a special friend with whom they can be totally honest, or to whom they can "sound off." Many believe that a spouse is one's best friend, but there is evidence that we all need a person with whom we can share our deepest longings, our highs, lows, doubts, fears, and convictions—and know that we'll still be loved.

I've been blessed with such a friend. When my stress quotient heads toward a new high, a conversation with my special friend puts things back into perspective. She may not always agree with my thinking that day; she may even be a little distant or preoccupied with her own problems, but most often she will be extremely sensitive, warm, and kind. I get the impression that she hurts when I do. I believe she often "travails" for me as Paul did for the brethren (Gal. 4). She listens, but not with the idea that she must get in her two cents. Sometimes she hears what I am *not* saying. My kind of high-pressure ministry would be impossible if God had not sent along this kind of a friend.

When it comes to friendships, women may have the advantage. They are more willing to share their problems and in that way reduce their stress. Friendships between men more often revolve around activities rather than sharing concerns, and this may account for why twice as many men as women are alcoholics. Men are taught to suppress their emotions and tend not to share their feelings.

In the Bible a friend is described as one who "loves at all times" (Prov. 17:17) and "sticks closer than a brother" (Prov. 18:24). Solomon describes a benefit of friendship: "Two are better than one, because they have a good return for their labor. For if either of them falls, the one will lift up his companion. But woe to the one who falls when there is not another to lift him up" (Ecc. 4:9-10). We also read in the Bible what it is like to be friendless. David did not always have his friend Jonathan. "I looked on my right hand and beheld, but there was no man that would know me . . . no man cared for my soul" (Ps. 142:4, KJV).

Job had "fair weather" friends who did him more harm than good.

Judas was an unfaithful friend to Jesus. How tragic when we realize what a good friend Jesus was. He said to His disciples, "No longer do I call you slaves, for the slave does not know what his master is doing; but I have called you friends, for all that I have heard from My Father I have made known to you" (John 15:15). To the disciples Jesus revealed information He gave to no one else. In His care and provision for them, He showed His love. In His contacts with Mary, Martha, and Lazarus we see how much He loved them, and how saddened He was when Lazarus died. Jesus even talked about giving our lives for our friends (John 15:13). David and Jonathan and Ruth and Naomi had special friendships. Their commitments were deep.

Friendship Requires Nurturing

I believe close friends can make or break our tolerance for stress in the '80s. It is my desire to be a buffer against the stress of our age to a few, close friends. We should not try to be *everybody's* friend. Intimate relationships require time and nurturing. We need to turn off activities and slow down so that we can "tune in" to one another.

A person may get 200 Christmas cards, but lack the intimacy of one or two special relationships. When one who has dozens of "friends" needs someone to talk to, he may realize his relationships are so superficial that he doesn't have a friend in the world.

Jesus knew the importance of spending more time with a few close friends and with His disciples. With those people He deepened His relationship and spent quality time.

One "sure thing" we can do to help others reduce stress is to listen. People are overcome by stress and anxiety because they have no one who will really listen to them. They often pay counselors to be their "professional listeners" when in some cases, an insightful listening friend could help a person as much as a psychiatrist. This is not to denounce counseling or psychotherapy. It is to say that many only need someone who will really listen to them.

Listening is fast becoming a lost art. It is a rare person who listens to a friend without thinking about what he is going to say next; who is thoroughly attentive. Few listen with eye contact; few listen for feelings, or for what is *not* said. Many look around when a friend is talking, or worse yet, at their watches as if to say they wish the conversation would speed up so they could move on to their next appointment.

Needed: Friends Who Listen

We are paying friends the highest compliment when we listen. We are letting them know what they say is important, that we value them and their thoughts. If they feel unheard, they may experience alienation, frustration, loneliness, or anger. We add to a person's stress when we don't listen.

In this age of mass communication, we can be reached with the flick of our television switches, but we cannot reach back. Only as we are able to make our feelings and thoughts understood can we form deep, personal relationships and be happier, healthier people.

Jesus was a good listener. "He asked questions of lepers, Roman officers, blind men, rabbis, prostitutes, fishermen, politicians, mothers, religious zealots, invalids, and lawyers. He wanted to hear the person before Him, and to know them as fully as possible" (Alan Loy McGinnis, *The Friendship Factor,* Augsburg, p. 112).

On several occasions I have experienced the healing power of a listening friend. Her eyes told me that what I was saying was of utmost importance to her. She drew me out and I talked about important matters that hadn't yet surfaced in my mind. She neatly and cohesively strung everything together so that what didn't even make sense to me, made sense to her. She often "plays back" what I say to find out what is going on inside me. She has the ability to make my anxiety float into insignificance because I am heard, loved, and understood.

And because God has always provided at least one of these friends, perhaps I have been spared the agony of alcoholism or serious neurosis. I want to play that role in the lives of a select few people and spare them the cost of intensive psychotherapy.

To get stress-relief from close friends, we must remember to be open. Too often there is the "trauma of transparency." Twentieth-century people are a real paradox: we long to reveal, and yet we generally conceal. We build up high walls and let few people, if any, inside those walls. We fear rejection should people really get to know us. We may long for intimacy and the close companionship of a friend, but unless we take off our masks, and are vulnerable, we'll have only casual, frustrating relationships that will do little to help us reduce stress.

Those who tell us we should not wear our emotions on our sleeves or that we should always keep a stiff upper lip are doing us no favor. Those philosophies try to make us ashamed of tears and deep emotions. Jesus wasn't ashamed of these. It has been said that we honor the person before whom we cry. That will usually deepen a relationship, as long as the tears aren't used in a manipulating way.

Laughter too is the world's best stress-reducer. Don't let your friendships or intimate relationships become so intense, serious, and introspective that they lack spontaneity and fun! See the humorous side of your friendships.

And since frustration and anger are emotions common to all, the best friendships will build in an allowance for negative feelings. There is no strong relationship that does not encounter some irritation at times, so agree early in your friendship that those feelings will be talked about and dealt with as they arise. Expect a few storms, but don't jump ship when they occur!

The climate should be such that you know you can say most anything to your friend. The words on a plaque in my office constantly remind me of this truth.

> Oh the comfort, the inexpressible comfort of feeling safe with a person; having neither to weigh thoughts nor measure words but to pour them all out, just as it is, chaff and grain together, knowing that a faithful hand will take and sift them, keeping what is worth keeping, and then, with the breath of kindness, blow the rest away. (George Eliot)

Stress-Producing Friendships

Friends can also produce intense stress by betraying a confidence, by talking behind our backs, or by making us feel guilty. Equally painful is a friendship gone sour due to possessiveness. This was the case of a friendship of mine many years ago. My friend and I had been college roommates and we shared similar interests, hobbies, and goals. Once out of college, we continued to play stress-reducing roles in one another's life.

But suddenly my friend became demanding of my time. She tried virtually to dominate me. She manipulated till she nearly suffocated me. What started out as a stress-reducing friendship turned into a nightmare that sent me to the hospital with stress-related symptoms.

"'At the heart of love,' some unknown sage wrote, 'there is a simple secret: The lover lets the beloved be free.' Those who have successful friendships allow their loved ones room. Rather than possessing their friends, they try to help them grow and become free" (McGinnis, *The Friendship,* p. 60).

So keep expectations realistic. Though we want closeness, we don't want to "smother" our friend. We don't want to come between a friend and her spouse, or between a person and God. There is a healthy balance between superficiality and an in-depth relationship.

For friendship to be stress-reducing it should bring out the best in one another (Prov. 27:17). It should draw us closer to God (Ps. 55:14). It should be compassionate but not encourage the "poor me" syndrome (Job 6), speak the truth in love (Prov. 27:6; Eph. 4:25), provide counsel from the heart (Prov. 27:9).

Friends must exercise a generous amount of forgiveness. When we're wrong, we need to say so. We need to take the initiative in forgiving our friends, to be able to bury the hatchet. We should drop all grudges into the deepest part of the ocean and plant a "no fishing" sign there. We must avoid the world's philosophy to "look out for number one."

Jesus taught that those who lose their lives will save them. He needs to be our pattern in relationships. And "from the time we see Him [Jesus] at the age of 12 in relationships, He is surrounded by persons with whom He forges a strong link. He opens Himself in a remarkable way to a number of intimates, and again and again we see Him extending Himself to take the initiative in loving others, doing favors for strangers, defending the disadvantaged, risking Himself for others when there is no possibility that He will ever reap anything from them" (McGinnis, *The Friendship,* p. 182).

If we handle them with care, our friendships can be the greatest buffer we have against the vicious onslaught of stress.

Help Us to Be Good Listeners, Lord

Lord, I've been talking all day,
    and not a soul has listened!
I've pleaded;
I've jumped on my bandwagon to preach
    and point fingers;
I've nearly begged for an audience,
    of even one person
    who will acknowledge my words.

Instead, my words have echoed noisily
    off of concrete buildings,
    and down dark alleys,
    and have come crashing back to me,
        unheard
            and
                unheeded.

Tomorrow I may try other tactics to be heard.
Perhaps a brass band;
Maybe a parade.

Couldn't we slow down just a little
    and quit running over people?
Instead spend time in the healing art
    of listening,
    thus saying
        you matter
        you count
        you have significance
        you have been heard
        you are important
        you have worth
            not just to God
            but to me.

Help us to be good listeners, Lord. Amen.

You're My Best Friend, Lord

You're my best friend, Lord.
With You I can risk everything.
I don't have to worry about
    measuring up
    or fitting in
    or looking just right
    or having the best clothes
    or saying all the right things.

I don't have to fear
    having a confidence betrayed
    or not being understood
    or being unable to keep up
        with the Joneses.

Our conversations are meaningful, Lord,
    and unlike so many,
    You listen,
        then listen again,
            and then again.
You give me Your undivided attention,
    and You never wonder how to break away
    lest You miss Your next appointment
And You are patient, Lord
    when I do all the talking.
You are faithful.
I can't turn You away.
You go on loving me
    in spite of traits
    that have turned others away.

Now may I be a friend to someone, Lord.
Show me the person who needs a good friend,
    and let me be the friend to them
    that You have been to me. Amen.

17
Stress and
the Elderly

Madison Avenue tries to convince us that we must buy a product because it will make us youthful, even if we're past middle age. The search for the fountain of youth continues as we hope that we will be the ones to find it.

Nevertheless, age—like old man river—keeps rolling along. Eventually eyes dim, hearing fails, and wrinkles deepen. The hair grays, the memory fades, and the body bends.

Though some may choose to isolate our elderly in nursing homes, God gives them a place of honor.

We are told to honor the elderly (Lev. 19:3).

King Rehoboam rejected the counsel of his old, wise men. Instead he listened to his young, inexperienced men, and as a result, Israel has been in trouble ever since (1 Kings 12). Older men and women such as Moses, Abraham, and Sarah accomplished great things for God in their later years.

The retired and elderly face tremendous stress from loneliness, poor health, and fixed or declining incomes. Their loved ones—spouses and friends—die. As the elderly fear uselessness and boredom, and become resigned to death, they hope it will come swiftly and painlessly lest they become a burden to family and friends.

If we learn to develop leisure activities *before* we retire or grow old, we will never be bored *after* retirement. Retirement can actually be a "commencement"—taking on life instead of taking it easy. The Department of Labor has revealed that people who retire with no planning have a life expectancy of 21 months beyond retirement. Those who voluntarily retire or utilize preretirement planning enjoy at least 13 years or more of productive life.

Apply Old Skills to New Activities

As you develop leisure skills, interests, and hobbies, it is important to look at the kinds of skills you now use in your life. Begin thinking how these can be applied to your retirement or nonwork related activities. For example, if you are a leader in business, you may want to continue developing leadership skills during retirement. If your hobby is travel, plan ahead for that trip of a lifetime that will make your retirement something to really look forward to. If creativity is your thing, pursue writing, art, or music in your senior years. Learn to play a new instrument, take up oil painting or ceramics.

There's a good chance that if you're a woman you may spend some of your golden years without your husband. Pensions and social security these days may not be enough for you. I know of four women, all over age 65, who began part-time careers in real estate, after 60. Begin to plan before retirement for such a vocation.

Retirement can open new opportunities to spend time with the Lord, with friends and with family, or to try a short-term missionary project. You might do volunteer work a day or two a week at a hospital or nursing home, or home for the handicapped. Your church probably has a dozen projects that you could head up.

We don't want to minimize the stress of the elderly and retired. As Christians we have a responsibility to them—to love them, pray for them, encourage them, and help them feel like productive, useful citizens. The church must reach out to these people and most are trying to do this. They have groups for outings and activities for seniors regularly. The church also needs to provide interaction between families and the elderly just as between the families and singles.

We are really only as old as we feel. If the older person is bored, it may be a problem of his own making. With planning, we can alleviate such stress-producers of old age as boredom, inactivity, and a feeling of uselessness.

Help Us to Be Unafraid, Lord

What paradoxes we are, Lord.
Within each of us is such a need
  to reveal
  and yet conceal.

A need to say,
  "I hurt"
  and yet communicate falsely,
  "I've everything under control."

A need to reach out and say,
  "Share my life, for I'm lonely"
  while we communicate,
  "I'm too busy to get involved with you."

A need to know You more intimately,
  and yet communicate
  spiritual indifference and complacency.

Help us to be unafraid, Lord,
  of ourselves
  and each other
  and You.

Help us to be real,
  and to accept each other
  in spite of ourselves.

Amen.

18
Stress and
the Christian Worker

A Christian counselor in Minneapolis has told me that stress casualties among Christian workers and leaders are high. He has some of the country's key Christian men and women as clients, many of them suffering from "burnout" and depression.

Pastors are particularly hard hit. Part of the problem stems from the fact that "we have deviated from biblical guidelines for churches and have instead created big buildings which sit empty for most of the week, superstar pastors who run a big organization, and passive congregations who come to be preached at and entertained" (Dr. Gary Collins, *You Can Profit from Stress,* Vision House, p. 178).

One minister recently polled the 28 officers in his church, asking them what they expected of him and how much time he should spend on activities such as sermon preparation, counseling, visiting the sick, etc. Eighteen of the 28 questionnaires expected the pastor to work more than 100 hours a week, and the average was 136.5 hours! If this man met the expectations of his people, he would have only 31.5 hours to himself all week, and if he used all of that time for sleeping, he'd get 4.5 hours per night! No wonder ministers feel stress. It can come from the people in his own congregation who pay him, in many cases, far less than they earn themselves in 35 and 40 hour a week jobs. . . . The [pastor's] hours are long, the pay is bad, the demands are great both on the minister and the family, and working conditions are frequently poor" (Collins, *You Can Profit,* p. 171).

In addition, the minister must help settle quarrels among the brethren and deal with crises in families—often at all hours of the day and night. He has committee meetings and administrative work (for which he may have little preparation or skill).

Christian workers are expected to be more spiritual than everybody else. Their family is to be a model to other families. They live a "fishbowl" existence. They often are expected to have answers to all of life's problems—even though their families are never to encounter any problems. They must know their Bible and provide the answers to all the theological questions that arise.

The stress of the missionary is also intense, and I speak from experience. I've been in evangelistic work for a number of years, but I know nothing of the tensions of the foreign field. Stress there is high as workers adjust to strange cultures, language barriers, and overwhelming work loads. Conditions are often difficult. The American dollar keeps devaluating, making their take-home pay less and less. They usually have little privacy and often lack recreation facilities. For many foreign missionaries, that stressful routine is broken only every four or five years when they are on furlough. Once home they must begin another stressful routine of traveling across the country to report to their backers and to raise more missionary support.

I get the impression that Christians expect me, as a worker in Jewish evangelism, to maintain a very proper image. At times I have wanted "to let my hair down" and I've received a look that said, "Are you sure missionaries should do that?"

Pressure from Supporters

Like every other missionary, I've traveled hundreds of miles raising support. Once it's been raised, I've had supporters remind me that I am to correspond with them frequently. In almost 10 years of missionary work, I've yet to be a part of a missionary board that sends out "prayer letters" which means I have to do the time-consuming correspondence myself and pay the postage for it. On one occasion I was scolded for sending only a Christmas card containing a brief note. Many supporters don't have these expectations, but the few who do cause heavy doses of stress.

I've been put on a pedestal by some Christians, and I've come crashing down more than once! Those situations put me under great stress. Trying to maintain any degree of perfection is exhausting!

However, all of us spreading the Good News should be concerned how we come across to those we're trying to lead into the kingdom. Whether we are with a tribe in a remote South American jungle, or the Jewish people in Minneapolis, we are always "on display." Our attitudes and reactions are being watched. We're ambassadors of the Living God and we do want to represent Him well! However, I always urge fellow workers in the ministry to show their normal feelings. Jesus let those He was trying to reach see His grief and His anger. I encourage Christian workers to stop trying to be all things to all people, and to refuse to let those whom they are serving "bleed them dry" with demands for ministry at any hour of the day or night. God is interested in the balanced life of the Christian in ministry as well as the Christian in secular work.

Casualty Rate Is High

I believe the family of God should help reduce the stress of those in full-time Christian service by encouraging them, praying for them, supporting them, and by not placing unrealistic demands and expectations on them. The casualty rate is high among pastors, missionaries, and Christian workers. Many missionaries come home before their furloughs for medical problems induced by stress. Depression and breakdowns are reported from every field.

Jesus said that "the Gospel will be preached in the whole world" (Matt. 24:14) and Christian workers are vital in carrying out God's plan, but if they burn out at an early age, what good are they?

Someday when I stand before the Lord and am commended for leading some souls to God, may it also be said that I never added to a fellow Christian worker's stress, that my expectations never drove anyone from the ministry, that I never discouraged my pastor or put unrealistic demands on him or his family.

Encounter

There was a time
  when I wept with
    every
      fallen
        leaf
  and barren tree.
When the chilly winds of November
  rang through the rafters in a minor key.
When flocks of birds flying south,
  took my heart with them.

But that was until the November day
  I
    met
      Jesus!

And now I leap into a pile of leaves;
Make angels in the snow;
Build canals in the March mud;
And have summertime in my heart year 'round!

19
Dealing
with Depression

Jonas Miller writes that about 80 percent of all people who go to the Mayo clinic for treatment are depressed, have nervous problems, or are trying to cope with situations they cannot master, and that most patients there are treated for physical diseases resulting from emotional frustration (*Prescription for Total Health and Longevity,* Logas, p. 46).

"Scientific research also shows that 85 percent of significant depressions are brought on by life stress" (Drs. Frank Minirth and Paul Meier, *Happiness Is a Choice,* Baker Book House, p. 98).

Depression is called the "common cold" of emotional disturbances. It is the leading cause of suicide, which is the 10th cause of death in America. A suicidal death occurs nearly every 20 minutes in the United States, and that doesn't take into account unsuccessful attempts. More than a half-million suicides are reported yearly from around the world (Minirth and Meier, *Happiness Is,* p. 31).

Doctors, nutritionists, counselors, and stress experts generally agree that depression is the sure sign that one's life is under stress and out of balance.

Depression hits the rich and the poor, and all ages. Women are treated twice as much as men, but our society encourages men to be "macho," to put up a brave front.

Unbalanced Lifestyle Causes Depression

Jane and I have experienced chronic depression brought on by the unbalanced lifestyle and I personally have spent thousands of dollars combating it. We know that the emotional pain of depression can be as severe as a broken arm or a migraine headache. We know that "a joyful heart is a good medicine, but a broken spirit dries up the bones" (Prov. 17:22).

My own depression was frequently brought on by my perfectionistic, workaholic lifestyle; by the repressing of natural emotions, by hanging on to feelings of unforgiveness, by harboring grudges.

And hand-in-hand were such comrades as anxiety, fear, worry, dread, tension, restlessness, concern, and general feelings of uneasiness. Because emotions produce illness, I experienced constant flare-ups of allergies, infections, and other sicknesses.

For some time I could not accept the diagnosis of depression handed to me by three doctors. I wanted them to write out a prescription for a "respectable illness," but instead I needed to deal with my emotions. And since I didn't have the insight or honesty to deal with them myself, I needed a counselor.

For too many years, seeing a counselor was shrouded in embarrassing overtones, even though "In abundance of counselors there is victory" (Prov. 11:14). Most of us would rather attribute the cause of our emotional problems to hypoglycemia or glandular disturbances, rather than admit that anger, unforgiveness, and other emotions are causes of stress and depression. Talking with a pastor, doctor, counselor, psychotherapist, or an insightful friend on a regular basis had a stigma, but it is gradually becoming respectable. Even Christian leaders are admitting their hurts and stresses. We're now a more "feeling-oriented" society; we're becoming more "up front" about a lot of things. Even churches are offering counseling programs and the waiting list is often long.

God did not correct my chronic, stress-induced fatigue till I dealt with the cause of that fatigue. Anger and resentment had brought on my serious depression. He was not going to relieve tension headaches till I attacked the depression and anxiety causing them. Unhealthy emotions were also affecting sleep, appetite, and even my posture.

Emotions were playing havoc with me physically. Depression was slowing the metabolism rate, causing a rapid heartbeat, intense restlessness, and an inability to concentrate. No number of physical tests was going to shed light on my depression and anxiety-induced symptoms.

Common Signs of Depression

In its mildest form, a depressed person may only feel "blue." At its worst, even the routine of dressing may seem impossible. Dr. William Backus of the Center for Christian Psychological Studies, St. Paul, Minnesota lists these signs of depression:

• A feeling of hopelessness, despair, or apathy. Feeling tearful, with little sense of humor. Every situation is recognized for its negative aspects. It is as though the depressed person had on negative "glasses" that eliminated everything positive from his sight. He often feels this condition will be permanent, with little hope for the future. Changes in physical conditions: sleep disturbances, eating too much or too little—usually too little, onset of mysterious pain (back, stomach, headaches), onset of unusual fatigue.

• Loss of self-esteem and frequently the onset of an unkempt appearance.

• Withdrawal from society—ranging from not returning phone calls to canceling activities and retreating to be alone as often as possible. Loss of interest in things that used to matter.

• Great difficulty handling feelings, especially anger.

• The onset of guilt feelings from assuming he is in the wrong and is responsible for making others unhappy.

• Oversensitivity to what others say and do, resulting in irritability.

• Expression of such statements as: "Nothing interests me anymore," "Life doesn't seem worth living," "I'd like to go to sleep and never wake up," "No one understands me," "I simply can't make up my mind anymore."

Telling depressed persons to "snap out of it" or "smile and you'll feel better" will do no good, so don't attempt it. Telling them they have nothing to be depressed about will make them feel even worse.

Instead get them to feel good about their strengths, their gifts and talents. Whenever they dwell on the negative, we should bring out the positive. The more we do that for them, the more they will be able to do it for themselves, eventually. Then we should reinforce their successes. We must be patient, remembering it took many years to develop this negative way of thinking and perceiving. It may not change overnight.

Drs. Frank Minirth and Paul Meier have written one of the best treatises on depression I've seen. *Happiness Is a Choice* is a manual of the symptoms, causes, and cures of depression. In it the authors conclude that "Most human depression is the result of our own irresponsible behavior . . . our own irresponsible handling of our anger and guilt. . . . The irresponsible actions of holding grudges is what brings on the majority of depressions" (p. 44). They believe nearly all depressions are brought on by pent-up anger, either toward ourselves or others. "Any accumulated grudges contribute to the biochemical changes that set up a depression" (p. 54).

Christians may have been told not to get angry. In Ephesians we read, "Be angry and yet do not sin; do not let the sun go down on your anger" (4:26). Though the Greek word translated "be angry" is in the imperative mood, it does not mean that we *must* be angry. Rather it is permissive, indicating we may be angry, but we should rid ourselves of hostilities as soon as possible—before the day ends!

Drs. Minirth and Meier maintain that "If Christians would maturely get rid of all grudges by bedtime, they would never become *clinically* depressed" (*Happiness Is,* p. 50).

I harbored anger against some former employers and against people who didn't "understand me" or agree with my theology and philosophy of life. I was angry at a friend who had misjudged my motives and who had betrayed me, and at former roommates. I held a grudge against a college professor whose grade had caused me to miss out on a much-needed scholarship. A best friend had moved on to be the best friend of another person and I harbored terrible feelings against her, though it had occurred 20 years earlier!

It seemed that with each new day came a new frustration. I buried the unhappy feelings under an already mile-high pile of emotional rubble. No amount of rest, relaxation, or leisure time eased the fatigue I had from repressing these feelings. I simply had to deal with them, and in my case, I got relief from a counseling program in a Christian clinic. When a sensitive, caring Christian counselor looked at the situations involved and when appropriate actions were taken to deal with my emotions, most of the remaining stress symptoms vanished within two months. Most important in the prescribed healing process was an attitude of love and forgiveness toward dozens of people.

I have always been impressed with a certain portion of the Jewish Passover Seder. At a designated point in the ceremony 10 drops of wine (symbolic of joy) are poured out in memory of the 10 plagues that befell the Egyptians. They decrease their joy in memory of what the Egyptians had to go through. What a lesson in forgiveness! Perhaps this is why the Passover celebration is such a joyful Jewish festival.

Jane Winn also speaks firsthand about depression. Her teenage and young adult years were unhappy and lonely, and she looked to drugs as an escape. When depression surfaced, three years of intensive psychotherapy were needed to bring her some stability. But still she had no inner peace. A Gentile Christian reached out to her and pointed her to salvation in the Jewish Messiah, Jesus. Till she gave her heart to Him at age 24, she remembers that she had experienced little, if any, joy—mostly sorrow and frustration.

When God touched her life, she distinctly felt He told her she would have the "gift of joy" and that she was to spread it among the heartbroken and depressed people she encountered. It was then she went to the mental health unit of a hospital, where she worked daily with chronically depressed patients.

She noted a pattern, particularly among Christian patients suffering from depression. Many of them could love their neighbor, but they couldn't love themselves. When they stumbled in their Christian walks, they didn't feel "good enough" to be Christians and became depressed. They were slaves to the "shoulds" of the Christian life (see chapter 3). Too often the patient had lost track of the grace message of the New Testament and focused on the Law of the Old Testament.

Some confessed that they felt like second-class Christians because they couldn't quit smoking, lose weight, or speak in tongues. Most often they had been encouraged not to express anger. They were constantly censoring themselves as Christians. Many were perfectionists and expected too much of themselves and others. Perfectionists have the highest rate of depression. A few were Christians in leadership who had been put on pedestals by other Christians. When they fell, they couldn't forgive themselves.

In most cases, the Christians she observed in the mental health unit were preoccupied with the way they were "supposed to be." In all instances the patients could not feel good about themselves. To the degree that Jane was able to help them focus on the "well" part of their personalities and like themselves, she saw signs of depression alleviate. Gradually the countenance and the color of their faces brightened, their appearances were neater, and postures more erect. Appetites returned to normal and they socialized spontaneously. Patients actually took risks with other patients.

Jane and I readily admit that the snare of depression always lies within our reach. It constantly lurks in a dark corner and would love to haunt us as long as we live. The minute our lives get out of balance, it tries to enter the picture. Every so often it makes temporary inroads—sleep is disturbed, and physical problems break out.

Dealing with Emotions

We must deal with emotions. But how? Do we dwell on them? Repress them? Throw "poor me" parties? Or do we confront them so we can move on and do the Lord's business? I hope the answer is obvious.

To defeat depression we must be in touch with our feelings and deal with them responsibly. In many cases the only way we can achieve this is through the insights gained in a counseling situation. If you think this is too expensive a way to cope with stress, you may find that it will be more costly *not* to do this.

Even though the authors have spent much of their lives dealing with depression, we are not experts on the subject. We don't want to simplify the problem, and we remind readers that depression can come from many sources. It may be the result of improper food or lack of rest, from a reaction to medications, from body infections or glandular disorders. Blood sugar problems can bring it on. We encourage you to see your doctor when the nagging symptoms of depression continue in spite of efforts to defeat it.

Remember that stress is a fact of life, and that stress management is *not* the process of eliminating all stress. Rather, it is choosing how to handle it.

Our bodies will tell us when we're undergoing too much strain and tension. Your stiff neck or headache will tell you when you're pushing your stress tolerance too far. Your indigestion will remind you that you can't "stomach" some situation in life. Your appetite problem will warn you when stress is "eating" at you. So listen to the warning signals your body sends out. Pay attention to your internal timing. Ask yourself, "How can I take better care of myself? What changes should I make in order that my body may more effectively glorify God?"

Stress can sometimes be an expression of God's love. Just as parents subject their children to stress to correct and discipline them, so God molds us in a similar way.

"We also know . . . that stresses sometimes bring glory to God, that they may come because of human disobedience . . . and that they can help us to develop patience. . . . They're something like surgery which hurts so we can get better" (Dr. Gary Collins, *You Can Profit from Stress,* Vision House, p. 217).

In the stress-saturated decade that lies ahead, remember that "His peace will keep your thoughts and your hearts quiet and at rest as you trust in Christ Jesus" (Phil. 4:7, LB).

Shattered Dreams Hurt, Lord

Lord, my dreams have turned to dust.
My hopes and aspirations have turned to ashes.
The road map to my life has hit a dead end.
You're the only One who can
    restore order to the confusion,
    direction to the wanderer,
    and purpose out of despondency and despair.

Shattered dreams hurt, Lord.
They take years to build,
    and only seconds to topple!
And now I'm back to zero.

But maybe that is where I need to be,
    in order to be pliable in Your hands.
To have nothing on earth to which I cling.
To abandon all the security blankets,
    and
        to
           let
               go
             into the safety net
                You have provided for me!

So I'll give You back the dreams, Lord,
    though I may put up a bit of a fight.
But take them
    and reshuffle my priorities,
    aspirations
    and longings of the heart,
    and make them in perfect accord
    with Your plan for my life!

Amen.

Selected prayers and poems
By Jan Markell

Rattle My Cage Gently, Lord

Lord, I'm caught in a rut!
I'm caught in a web of routine . . .
So comfortably swallowed up in the
  status quo
  to ever conceive of new horizons;
Drowning in the comfort of the familiar,
  feeling far too safe to
    risk
    or reach out to
      new friends
      new ideas
      or new ways of doing old things,
And feeling too spiritually lethargic to
  step out in faith
  yield to You bad habits
  or attitudes
  or weaknesses
  or prejudices.

Rattle my cage gently, Lord!
I tread lightly through new circumstances.
But rattle it if You must.
I know You will be there when I break out,
  and that You will lead me
    down
      new
        and
          exciting
            pathways
              of
                life!

Amen.

Reality Is Frightening, Lord

Lord, it seems that life
Is a series of events
For which we must learn to cope.
   Stress factors
   Breaking points
   Anxiety attacks
Are becoming fashionable words
And a way of life.

We can talk of the good old days;
Nostalgia can lull us to sleep,
But reality is all too often
Enveloped in a dark cloud,
Shrouded in shades of gray
And often as exhilarating
As dense fog on a freeway.

Reality is frightening, Lord.
A variety of "isms" threaten my very being,
And what is worse,
Threatens and attempts to corrode
Everything I believe in.

Father, I need Your hand of assurance.
I need to know You have everything under control.
I need to lean on You,
And be told, like a child,
That everything will be alright.

Forgive this childish insecurity;
Help me to rest upon Your promises,
And dwell peacefully in Your love;
To claim the victory in life,
And to hang on to Your strength.

Amen.

Faces

Faces . . .
   haunting
     helpless
       hopeless
Reaching out
Yet backing away.

Faces . . .
   wearing smiles,
   but beneath,
     uncertainty
       loneliness
         alienation
           apathy.
Faces . . .
   in a crowd,
Mistaking noise for laughter
And elbows for hands
And shoves for a pat on the back.

Father,
Help us see the heart,
And meet a need,
Fill a void,
Be a friend.
Don't let us drown in complacency . . .
Snug in our circle,
Secure in our niche,
While those around us
Hear our words about
   love
     and
       compassion
Bounce off empty walls
And have no more meaning
Than the headline on a movie magazine.

Amen.

These Are Staggering Times, Lord

These are staggering times, Lord!

Dollar devaluation and mushroom shaped clouds
Cause us to grope frantically
For a security blanket!

Do You chuckle as You see us seek safety in
    financial nest eggs
    retirement plans
    and investment opportunities?
Or enter into the escape tactics of
    clubs, causes, crowds,
    amphetamines or barbituates,
    or mind-paralyzing tube watching?

Life is full of escape hatches
    and cop-out opportunities
But they last only until the next crisis develops.

Lord, help us to rest securely in You
Help us to latch onto the life-jacket You've tossed out,
And to ride the waves,
Safe in Your loving protection
Secure in the midst of earthly peril,
Confident in Your care,
Assured of Your control,
    in an angry,
        explosive
            world!

Amen.

Curtain Call

It seems it's true . . .
All the world's a stage
Upon which masked actors
Perform carbon-copy tragedies
With few comedies,
And the curtain falls too soon,
And few live happily ever after.

It seems everyone is late,
Or off to the mad hatter's tea,
And wishing they, like Alice
Were just dreaming,
And soon, reality would bring safety.

Funny thing is . . .
It only gets worse,
And man continues on a
   non-stop
   one-way
   collision-course to hell.

But the One who offers peace,
The One who offers hope
And the One who offers reality,
Tarries a bit longer
To write the last act
So that just one more
Might escape the absurd
And enter a heavenly shelter
Where the curtain will fall forever
   on masks
   and costumes
   and bad scripts
   and unhappy endings.

OVERCOMING STRESS

JAN MARKELL

While this book is designed for the reader's personal enjoyment and profit, it is also intended for group study. A Leader's Guide with Victor Multiuse Transparency Masters is available from your local bookstore or from the publisher.

VICTOR BOOKS

a division of SP Publications, Inc.
WHEATON. ILLINOIS 60187

Offices also in Fullerton, California • Whitby, Ontario, Canada • Amersham-on-the-Hill, Bucks, England

Poems between chapters and at the end of the book are by Jan Markell and are part of collections entitled *Peace Amidst the Pieces* and *Somebody Loves Me*. Used by permission of Adventure Publications, Staples, Minnesota.

Most of the Scripture quotations in this book are from the *New American Standard Bible* (NASB), © 1960, 1962, 1968, 1971, 1972, 1973 by The Lockman Foundation, LaHabra, California. Other quotations are from the *King James Version* (KJV), the *New International Version* (NIV), © 1978 by the New York International Bible Society, and *The Living Bible* (LB), © 1971 by Tyndale House Publishers. Used by Permission.

Recommended Dewey Decimal Classification: 614.582.2
Suggested Subject Headings: STRESS: ANXIETY

Library of Congress Catalog Card Number: 81-86290
ISBN: 0-88207-319-2

VICTOR BOOKS
A division of SP Publications, Inc.
P.O. Box 1825 • Wheaton, Illinois 60187